Revelations

A Survivor's Story of Faith, Hope and the Coming Kingdom

Nicole DiCenzo

Cover custom photography provided by Jessica Flynn of Capture Photography.

Back cover photography also by Jessica Flynn of Capture Photography. www.capturephotosite.com

Note: The smoking boots shot on the back represents the rapture!

For my Daddy and my Jesus,
thank You for Your love and sacrifice.
May these words bring You glory.

To my husband, Doug,
I love and miss you.
Hurry Up!

Special thanks to: My Battalion
(see page 131 at back).
A special, special thanks to
those who have helped bring about
this book: Amanda, Jess,
Roger, and my mom.
I love you all.
nic

To the Reader:

My name is Nicole DiCenzo; my friends call me Nic. The story you are about to read is my story. I have lived these words over and over. They are as true as I can represent them on paper.

Although this is my story, it is also God's story, because this is the story He has graciously chosen for my life. His Word has the words that bring life. May you find hope in His Word, as have I.

My husband's name is Doug DiCenzo. This is also his story, yet I cannot tell you if his perspective in this story is completely accurate. He is with Jesus, and the words he speaks in this narrative have played out since his death. Although I have represented his time in Heaven based on scripture, many details are rooted in my own imagination. Please note the scripture references and use them as needed.

As you turn these pages, may God give you wisdom and revelation. However, I must warn you, God's revelation brings many revelations, and revelations can change your life.

They have changed mine.

Nic

CHAPTER ONE

Forsaken

"My God, my God, why have you forsaken me? Why are you so far from saving me, so far from the words of my groaning?"

Psalm 22:1

*D*oug didn't feel the explosion. All he saw was a flash of light and a multitude of angels fading in through the smoke and cinders until they were clear and bright, like an all-consuming flame. With slight wonder Doug realized they had been there all along, letting nothing happen to destroy those things God wanted preserved from the prevailing evil of the day.

They came in quickly, diving forward, arms stretched out, chiseled faces tight with resolve. One led the way, curly chocolate brown hair streaming behind him like a war banner, midnight eyes focused intently on his target.

Doug faltered as the ramifications became clear. He thought of his son Dak, only sixteen months old.

Then he thought of Nic.

It seemed like only yesterday he had bowed to one knee and asked her for her hand in marriage. Now, over six years later, they were still just as happy. Whenever Nic saw an elderly couple holding hands she would lean close and whisper, "That's us when we get old, Doug."

But the angels.

They advanced swiftly, their brilliant white garments curving around their bodies as they steadied their decent. Muscular frames ranging from slender to robust were tense with conviction. They were all vastly different, yet each of them had the same fierce resolve, the same surety of purpose, and the same concentrated piercing gaze. The lead angel's midnight eyes captured Doug's attention. They bore through him with an understanding so vast that Doug felt his spirit shiver. This angel was the first to reach him and the first to grip his soul.

He thought of Nic and her dream of holding hands when they grew old and for a brief moment his spirit protested the angelic escort, but their grip was too certain, their silence too stark, and their urgency far too real.

They set their sights skyward, never once hesitating in their flight. Their firm hands gently gripped what were now his arms. Their silence stood in stark contrast to the fiery inferno below.

He saw his vehicle burning as another small explosion resonated in the afternoon air. His soldiers sprinted toward the blaze, shouting his name, but knowing they were too late. Their commanding officer was gone.

Doug wanted to reassure them but his voice wouldn't come. The sorrow emanating from the angels tore him to the core. They mourned for him even as they directed him from the blaze. He could hear their silent words, "How long, O Lord, holy and true, will you refrain from judging those who dwell on the Earth?"[1]

They rocketed skyward until the smoke from the blaze was a distant dream. Starlight streaked by him, cutting the blackness like thin knives.

A brilliant light appeared above him. Within moments, it encompassed everything in his vision. Doug tried to look back but the stars were either no longer there or hidden by the light. Its brilliance was brighter than anything he had ever known yet it contained no glare or heat. It was a fire's flame without consumption, a volcano's intensity without destruction. It was consuming but not crushing.

When Doug's eyes shifted to the source of the light, his fears evaporated like dew in the desert. He didn't recall the angels melting away or the seconds that led him there. He didn't even recall the explosion. Every thought was focused on the spellbinding figure before him.

Jesus.

The Lamb was robed in white linen with a golden sash loosely draped around His waist. His rich velvet hair danced with starlight and His face radiated a thousand suns. His dark eyes were intense, yet gentle, and His smile reflected a love so vast the blackest night could not conceal it.

The scars on His hands and feet were plainly visible, almost a black hole in the crystal clear brilliance, yet those scars sent the already glorious light into spectrums of color. The understanding in the lines of His face was far deeper than the angels', so much so that when Jesus looked at him, Doug was known, as he had never been known before. Every emotion he had felt, every thought he had pondered, every deed he had done lay naked and exposed before the One who cast the stars in the sky.

Doug fell to his knees, overcome with the knowledge of God. He was but a grain of sand, one created being in untold billions. How did he come to capture the favor of God?

"What is man that you are mindful of him, the son of man that you care for him?"[2]

The Word came to him easily, as if he had recited it by memory hundreds of times before. The Spirit was alive here, unhindered by human desires and the enemy's tactics. It flowed through his veins and brought to mind verses that wrapped him in vast reassurances of his Savior's love.

He felt his tears come without any reservation. The spectrums of light radiating from his Savior's nail scared feet washed through Doug with overwhelming compassion. He was clean, washed by the blood of the Lamb. He heard his voice whispering a heartfelt thanks. Without Jesus' sacrifice on the cross the angels wouldn't have come for him. Without Jesus there would have been no hope at all.

Jesus placed a firm hand on his shoulder, "Well done, my child."[3] It was the voice that commanded the light to form, the sound of a rushing river, a coming train, thunder without lightning, an earthquake without destruction. It could make the sun shrivel and the moon explode yet it was as a feather on his cheek and dew on the wings of an eagle. It was power, yet it was love. That was the voice of his Savior. It was the voice that would one day command the dust that was now his body to take to the sky. The light, the peace, and Jesus' mere presence filled every part of Doug's spirit without any weight.

There was no weight here.

Doug blinked back tears as he thought of Nic. The weight she would now carry would threaten to crush her.

Jesus tightened His grip, halting any anxious thoughts. Doug lifted his eyes to his Savior. Jesus smiled. The light emanating from His face became a crown, a silent witness to the promise of His coming reign. Doug couldn't form the words to express the reassurance he felt. No amount of evil in this world could stop his King from coming; no amount of destruction Satan's minions could unleash would hinder the millennial reign of Christ.

"Thy kingdom come," was in the Lord's Prayer, but not many people realized what those words truly meant.

"Amen and amen," Doug said. "Come quickly, Lord Jesus."[4]

෧෨

When the knock sounded on my door I thought it was one of the girls in the apartment complex coming to watch the finale of *American Idol* with Jan and me.

When Doug obtained orders to report to Baumholder, Germany we were given housing on an off-post military complex situated in the quaint town of Birkenfeld. Of the ten military families living in the complex, nine of the wives, including myself, had remained in Germany when our husbands deployed to Iraq. Although many of us didn't know each other well until our husbands left, the building had become like a college dorm, each of us moving between apartments to help pass the day.

The knock came for the third time. I turned to Jan in slight confusion. "Why don't they come in?"

Jan was one of my closest friends in the complex. Although a decade younger, our bubbly personalities fit well together. People heard us before they saw us. My loud bullet-style giggle along with her boisterous laugh turned heads. I knew whoever was at the door had heard my invitation. I didn't understand why they didn't come in.

When I opened the door I came face to face with two soldiers in full military uniform.

If you're a military wife you know why they have graced your doorstep. You have had nightmares of their knock. You fear their words. When you allow yourself to imagine that day, you cry. It is part of the world in which you live. It is hell.

Almost exactly one-year prior, Doug had told his superiors he wanted to be stationed in Baumholder, Germany with 2-6 Infantry. They were the unit scheduled to deploy to Iraq.

I didn't want to move to Baumholder. If Doug took command there he would deploy for at least a year. 2-6 was scheduled to leave for Iraq in November. Our son had just been born in January. I wanted Doug home, as most wives would, but it wasn't my decision to make.

I still remember our conversation. Dak was on my lap, just a few days old. Doug was on leave in celebration of Dak's entrance to the world.

"I want to go to Baumholder, to 2-6 Infantry," Doug said. "I think that would be a good unit and a good area."

"Isn't that unit deploying?" I asked.

Doug looked at me with his soft brown eyes. "Yes."

I had fallen in love with those eyes. They were honest, kind, and always had a smile flickering in their depths.

"Doug, you could be killed."

"It's rare when a leader is out in front," he said. "I'll be okay."

"Doug," I said again, "You could be killed."

"But I won't be."

I knew he was just telling me what I wanted to hear. I was scared, but it wasn't my decision to make. I left it up to him.

"Nic," he said, "one day or another I will deploy to Iraq. It might as well be now."

I didn't understand. Most wives wouldn't. I would never want to leave my family for a year, but it wasn't that Doug wanted to deploy, it was that he felt a duty to his country and to the soldiers already overseas. At times I didn't like Doug's sense of duty, and this was one of those times. But I understood his mind. Soldiers were in Iraq and he wasn't with them. Soldiers were dying and he wasn't there. America was at war and he hadn't been called. "Duty, honor, country," was the motto of West Point, the military academy where Doug graduated. If anyone in the world embodied those three words it was Doug, and although I hated it, I also knew that was why I loved him.

Doug felt a duty to go. He needed to go. He had to go.

Now Doug would never come back.

I turned to Jan who had risen from the couch. Her eyes were wide and her hand was clinched over her gaping mouth. The shock in her face sent a dagger into my already shattered heart.

"Jan?" I said in desperation.

My mind went into overdrive. I was out of body, floating. I was in the scene but not of the scene. I wanted to run but there was nowhere to go. I felt awkward. I kept turning back to Jan. Time seemed to stop.

I remember looking at each man's face thinking, *"No, no, this can't be. Doug isn't dead. That's impossible. If he was I wouldn't be able to breathe. I would be on my knees. I would be doing something, not just standing here. I would be screaming."*

"Mrs. DiCenzo?"

I wanted to stop the man's words, push them back into his mouth and close the door, but I did not. I just stood there, speechless and shattered.

"Your husband was killed today in Bagdad, Iraq."

Doug could feel the aftershock as the news of his death reached Nic's door. He could sense Nic's devastation almost as if he were standing right beside her, telling her himself.

The Savior's arm that encircled Doug's shoulder tightened its grip, and as Nic's inner scream surfaced visions pelted Doug's conscious: an earthquake, a dark sun, a red moon; the blast of the shofar, Nic's joyful cry, his urn toppling, ashes bursting skyward; a white horse, a red rose and an embrace.[5]

Then laughter, more glorious laughter than he had ever heard before.

Engulfing him.

Flooding his lingering pain with hope.

As quickly as the visions had come they were gone, but in their wake was complete peace.

The Savior standing beside him cast every doubt aside. One day soon, justice would be served, both to the righteous and the wicked.

Nic knew that too. She was already praying. He could feel her words drifting up like fragrant incense to the altar of God.[6]

"And will not God bring about justice for his chosen ones, who cry out to him day and night? Will he keep putting them off? I tell you, he will see that they get justice, and quickly."[7]

"Her road will be hard," Jesus said, "but the Spirit will guide her, step by step, into the truth she will so desperately seek."

Doug nodded in gratitude as a joyful cry screamed in his soul. Nic wanted what he wanted. She wasn't about to let him go. He could already feel Nic's heart reaching out to God. What was Heaven, she asked? What would it be like? Look like? Feel like?

Would she ever be able hold his hand again?

Grateful tears welled in Doug's eyes. Her dream of holding hands would never diminish. It would only intensify with each day apart.

"I will protect her from attack for a season," Jesus said. "When her screaming abates we will assure her what the Spirit is telling her is the truth."

❦

As the notifying soldiers flanked me on the couch, I kept glancing at the picture I had propped up in my entertainment center. It was a close up of Doug holding Dak while we were hiking in Garmisch, Germany prior to Doug's deployment. We had stopped to eat a picnic lunch beside an isolated mountain lake that reflected the fall foliage. The moment was captured perfectly. Doug wore his dark khaki shirt zipped to the top and Dak had on a bright blue fleece jacket that said "daddy and me." Doug hadn't shaved that day and his shadow was heavy. There was a big grin on his face and, as always, his eyes were smiling. Those eyes smiled at me now as I sat on the couch. As I looked at that picture, so alive and vibrant, it was impossible to comprehend what the notifying officers were saying. Doug was alive, more alive than anyone I knew.

The men remained beside me. I wanted them to leave but I didn't know how to speak the words to force them out my door. They slowly reviewed what would happen the next day. I would meet my Casualty Assistance Officer, the CAO, and he would help me sift through the ramifications of Doug's death.

My mind still could not grasp it.

I looked up at Jan, hovering a short distance away, staring at me with her hand still clasping her mouth, eyes still wide with the same emotions that screamed in my chest.

"Get Tara," I said. Tara was my other close friend in the complex. Tara would know what to do. Tara always knew what to do.

Why don't the men leave? I thought. *And why wasn't I crying?* I suddenly realized I wasn't crying.

Sweet Jesus, my sweet Lord Jesus, why am I not crying?

"I can't cry." It was a shocked statement. These men had just told me Doug had been killed. I wanted to cry, to show the world how much I loved him. Why wasn't I crying?

"That's natural," the soldier said who gripped my hand. "You're in shock."

"You're in shock, Nic," Tara repeated, nodding in agreement. I hadn't heard her come in, or had I? I couldn't recall. I looked up at her, trying to shout with my eyes to help get the men out of my apartment. Tara could do that; she could fix it; but Tara looked stricken, like she had been punched in the gut. I could see the concern in her eyes. She was dying for me.

I sat on the couch thinking an eternity had crept by but in actuality it was only a few minutes.

"Do you want your chaplain to come in?" the officer asked.

I didn't know, but I did want the men beside me to leave. They kept asking if I had any questions or if there was someone I wanted them to call.

"No," I said. I had thought this through. I knew the order of those I needed to call. I couldn't imagine Doug's parents getting the news over the phone from a stranger. Maybe that's what prompted me to tell the men to leave.

Moments after the door clicked shut Dak started crying. The house was quiet, and he shouldn't have woken. It was only nine o'clock at night and my sixteen-month-old was a good sleeper.

"He senses something's wrong," Tara said. "Do you want me to get him?"

I shook my head "no." I could almost feel Tara's oozing concern and Jan's continued shock. My tears still hadn't come so Dak was crying for me.

"Poor Dak," I said, sudden terror gripping me. Doug had said goodbye when Dak was only ten months old. "Poor Dak," I said again. It was something I would repeat over and over the next few days.

Tara's response was always the same, "No, Nic. He has you."

But he didn't have Doug, and Doug was a much better person than me. At times he came home telling me about something he alone had done for the sake of the unit. When approached by those higher up Doug would always reply "the unit" did this or that. I would shout in outrage, "No, you did it! No one helped you!"

"It's a team effort," he would always reply. I could only stare. What kind of person was this who did something by himself and gave the credit to the team?

I don't remember walking to Dak's room, but I remember picking him up and telling him how sorry I was. I stood there holding my child with the sudden realization that Doug was gone. The house was quiet but I was not. Inside, I was screaming.

When someone tells you they are screaming inside believe them. Out of everything I experienced the scream was the most bizarre, the most devastating, yet the most liberating expression of pain I experienced. I heard my own voice as clear as crystal, I felt my lungs expand as if a scream would explode from my lips, but my lips never moved and no breath ever escaped my lungs. Yet the scream was all encompassing and total. I found myself screaming even when others were surrounding me. It was a constant presence in my life for almost a year.

My movements that night were awkward and planned. I had to think to myself "move" before my legs would start to work. Things surrounding me were surreal, almost time warped. I was unaware of the minutes ticking by or the whispers that surely emanated from the living room. Every muscle was on alert, yet my mind was delayed.

Karen, another friend in the complex, came soon after I checked on Dak. Hard as steel, we lovingly referred to Karen as the "crusty old hag" despite her young age, so when Karen hugged me it was almost out of character. She brushed my hair as I stood there awkwardly, telling her I couldn't cry. Karen said

I was crying in ways I couldn't see, and she was right. My scream was a cry and so was my shock, but I didn't realize it at the time.

Then I sat at my dining room table with my friends surrounding me. I remember someone handing me the phone and someone else retrieving my address book. I remember shaking, trying to find the right phone numbers. I needed to call Doug's stepfather first. I knew Doug's mother needed Mark to be with her when the news came. I had even asked Doug before he left for Iraq if I had made the right decision. He assured me I had.

I think Mark knew as soon as he heard my voice. "Doug didn't make it," I said.

He sighed heavily and said, "Nic, I'm so sorry."

I knew he was sorry, as everyone would be, but from Mark it meant a lot. Mark was a rare person, sarcastic and cryptic, yet when you peeled away the hard shell there was a man who would do anything for you. He had never had children of his own, and had married Cathy when Doug was twelve and Doug's brother Dan was nine. He stood behind in the shadows for years, always there for Doug and Dan, yet understanding he could never take the place of their father. Doug admired him a great deal, and because Mark had never had any children of his own, Doug and I decided to name our son after Mark: Dakin Mark DiCenzo.

I'm glad we made that decision because it's a testimony to Mark, as well as every other male influence in Dak's life, that Dak needs the men surrounding him to help shape his world view, men who will be friends, yet also understand that "no" is not a negative word. The grandparents in Dak's life don't have the privilege of being that "fun grandparent." They have the responsibility of shaping a young mind who has lost one of the most influential people in his life.

The next call was to Doug's father. Larry is Italian, a man of great emotion who doesn't allow himself to show it. Larry is quiet, but also the life of the party. And he loves his boys. You could see the pride in Larry's eyes whenever he heard Doug's name. That was his son, Doug, who had gone to West Point, who had committed his life to the army, who was one of the best men any father could hope to have as a son.

"Doug didn't make it," I said.

I couldn't say "killed" or "dead" to Doug's parents. I still can't say those words today. They leave me bone dry. Although my husband was killed, he is not dead. He is waiting in Heaven with Jesus. One day I will see him again.

Larry's reaction tore me even more than Mark's. "What?" he screamed.

I had to repeat myself although I knew he had heard me clearly. I still remember Larry's scream. I remember putting my hand to my mouth and whispering how sorry I was.

Then I called my parents. I don't remember what either of them said because an enormous wave of anxiety had started to dissolve. I had been worried about Doug's parents, and now my parents could worry about me. That is what parents were supposed to do, and that is what I knew they would do. Although my parents divorced when I was two, they had always been on speaking terms. My parents immediately started searching for flights to Germany. They would arrive at my door in approximately thirty-six hours.

Then Doug's mother called. Cathy's first words were, "He didn't mean to hurt you this way."

No, Doug didn't, and I knew that, but it was still good to hear. Doug was the protector of men and the protector of me. One time on a kayaking trip in Alaska, I was terrified of the frigid water, tense, and ready to get to shore. If you flipped over in Alaska's water it only took twenty minutes for hypothermia to set in.

"Don't worry," Doug said, "I won't let anything happen to you."

Now the absolute worst had happened and Doug wasn't there to reassure me, but his mother's words did. "He didn't mean to hurt you this way."

Slowly, the hours rolled by and my friends began to leave. I lay on the couch at three o'clock in the morning and started to sob. As the internal scream grew louder, slowly, ever so slowly, it started forming a prayer.

"Daddy, help me. Please Daddy, help me. Daddy, help me." I repeated it over and over. At times, I'm sure those words passed through my mind hundreds of times in an hour. They were a constant presence, a security blanket that I clung to when I felt myself gasping for air.

I had never called God "Daddy" before. God the Father had always been slightly elusive to me. Jesus I could touch and feel, His sacrifice brutal yet beautiful. But God? Who was He? That night I discovered who God really was and His new name rolled off my tongue like butter.

Daddy.

This epithet should've come as no surprise. Galatians 4:6 says, *"Because you are sons, God sent the Spirit of his Son into our hearts, the Spirit who calls out, "Abba, Father!"*

I knew in my heart that everything would be okay because Daddy was with me. He was a father that yearned for His child to run into His open arms.

And run I did, with full force. I could almost feel my hands clinching His garment, holding onto the truths He had inundated my world with over the past five years.

Doug is not dead, I told myself, *because Jesus is not dead.*

Within heartbeats I understood the significance of the Savior I had always believed in. I knew mentally what Jesus' sacrifice ultimately meant, but I hadn't internalized it. Jesus had conquered death so my husband could live. My husband was not dead. One day, I would see him again. My Daddy and my Jesus would make sure of that.

Daddy. It fit Him that night. It still fits Him today. God loves us, like a loving earthly father.

"The Lord your God is with you, he is mighty to save. He will take great delight in you, he will quiet you with his love, he will rejoice over you with singing."[8]

Daddy knew I needed saving. I needed Him to quiet me with His love. I needed the screams to eventually stop.

Although I didn't sense God that night, couldn't find Him in my immeasurable pain, I knew He was there. By Daddy's grace and love He had strengthened my faith for that hour. Over the days that followed my screams continued to magnify that prayer.

In my human emotions I felt alone. On the cross Jesus felt alone too as He called out with excruciating passion, *"My God, my God, why have you forsaken me?"*[9]

My pain can't compare to what Jesus experienced but I felt that same cry, and with that cry Daddy gave a promise: *"Call upon me in the day of trouble; I will deliver you, and you shall glorify me."*[10]

Call on Him I did. The screams continued, and with each expansion of my lungs, with each heartbreaking tear, and with each agonizing breath I knew Daddy was right there. He would not forsake me. He would come when I could hear.

The strange thing was I had known in my heart, in my gut, four months prior that Doug wasn't coming home. Daddy had prepared me for it. I knew it, yet I had pushed it out of my mind, being reassured by my friends that I was just being frantic.

But Daddy has His ways, and without those preparations my dark world would have been much darker. Without my previous sorrows I may not have stood in Daddy's strength at all.

&

Before Doug could ask how Nic would be protected, and what the Spirit would do to reassure her, he suddenly realized he was standing alone.

Doug surveyed the valley in which he stood, but he saw no sign of Jesus. In the distance majestic mountains rose from the valley floor and a large waterfall cascaded down one side into an enormous crystalline lake. Mist from the falls swirled skyward, shrouding the mountains in a glorious haze.

The colors here were dazzling, as if all his life he had been looking through a smoky veil. The blues were bluer, the whites were purer, and the greens, well, they were alive. As Doug continued to study his surroundings he became aware of colors he had never seen before. The tiny flowers dotting the grass weren't orange, yet they weren't quite pink. The grass itself had a glow to it, like it had been nourished with liquid gold. Doug reached out and brushed the grass, marveling at how God's unending light reflected off each individual blade. The saints, he supposed, cast God's light in a similar way. Each individual reflected God's glory, yet as a whole, they magnified His light with breathtaking clarity.

Doug studied his hand, somewhat stunned. Although he had never dwelt on what Heaven would be like he had always assumed he would be a spirit here. Doug clinched his fists, feeling the familiarity of the body he now wore. It was as if Father had made him a second skin so he would be able to enjoy Heaven. It was him, yet it wasn't the body Nic had touched. It was a temporary dwelling, one that would dissolve at the sound of the shofar and the call of his Savior. At Jesus' command, his old self, now ashes, would become new again.[11] He would have his old skin back, yet it would be reborn, glorified, and fit to live for eternity. His mind could scarcely grasp it.

As more questions surfaced, they faded to a mere afterthought. The absolute authority of the Father and the love of his Savior were in the air he breathed, moving through him like living water, cool, refreshing, and full of hope. Although some questions remained, he knew their answers would be perfect because he was in the hands of a completely loving God.

Doug leaned his head back and drank in God's glorious light. As his questions stilled the silence surrounding him slowly began to form distinct voices. When he turned to the sound, there before him, rising from the valley floor like a cedar in the desert, was the New Jerusalem.

It shone like a diamond had engulfed the sun. Light emanated from its multifaceted sides as if the stars themselves lived there. Biblical knowledge of Revelation leapt into his conscious as if he were a learned scholar that had poured over the Word for centuries. As his eyes swept the walls of the city the description he had read only once before sharpened and intensified.

Twelve gates, each formed by a single pearl, were set in the surrounding walls and shimmered like the moon had come to rest in twelve different places. The walls' twelve foundations glistened with every gem imaginable: jasper, sapphire, chalcedony, emerald, sardonyx, carnelian, chrysolite, beryl, topaz, chrysoprase, jacinth, and amethyst. Each layer lifted the city higher, floating it on an ocean of color. On the foundations were the names of the twelve apostles of the Lamb.[12]

The city itself was a square, as long as it was high and wide. The streets of the city were paved with pure gold as transparent as glass in the ocean. The beauty of it took Doug's breath away. He took a step toward the gates, a sudden urge to draw closer to the God that had graciously sent His only Son to die for his sake.

As he listened, the distant voices became clear: "Holy, Holy, Holy is the Lord God Almighty, who was, and is, and is to come!"[13]

Doug inherently knew those voices came from the four creatures surrounding the throne of God. They never ceased their unending song. When their words ended they began again, and with each utterance the truth of their declaration settled in Doug's conscious with rock solid surety.

Doug began to run through golden green grass as an insurmountable joy bubbled inside him. The words of the creatures resonated inside him as if he had been waiting for this day and this day alone.

He was born for eternity, for this; he existed to serve his God in the great city rising before him.

Out of the corner of his eye, he saw an angel move above him, flying from the Earth to deliver a message to his Father.

Jesus' words came rushing back.

"I will protect her from attack for a season."

With sudden understanding, Doug stopped as the messenger of the Lord surged past him, his startlingly white linen garments mirroring the same radiance as the distant city. The angel paused in his flight, chocolate brown hair curling around his neck and his garments billowing around his form with rare beauty.

As the creature moved closer, Doug realized it was the same angel who had first gripped his soul and ushered him to Heaven. The angel's eyes held the knowledge of ages, but in them was something Doug was unprepared to see – urgency.

There was nothing urgent about Heaven; everything here was peaceful, yet the angel carried with him a yearning for haste.

The angel's lips pursed and his midnight eyes grew fierce as they reflected the intensity of the explosion that had taken Doug's life.

The loyalty in the angel's eyes was awe-inspiring. No soldier on Earth had that kind of devotion. The force of it radiated from the angel as if an emotion could have a color all its own.

As they continued to study one another a familiarity grew inside Doug. He knew this creature. His realization caused the angel to smile. Doug couldn't help but grin back, almost giddy with his Father's love. This angel had been assigned to him since he was a child and had followed Doug during life under the direct order of God.[14]

When his life had ended on Earth, the angel before him had instantly gone to Nic's side. The creature's stern gaze not only emanated a rage of Doug's death but also an intense loyalty to the woman Doug loved.

"She will run with perseverance the race marked out for her."[15] The angel's deep voice danced into Doug's soul, causing his insides to quake with the majesty of God's creation. The angel's voice itself was worship. One word from his lips and God was praised.

In the distance the creature's voices lifted higher, mightier and with more intensity. The angel turned his gaze to the city of God, midnight eyes hardening in resolve. The loyalty Doug had sensed previously faded in comparison to the devotion the angel emitted as it looked toward its Creator. The spellbinding beauty Doug had seen moments prior could be nothing more than rubbish as the creature shifted its thoughts toward Jesus.

The angel's deep voice once again reverberated inside Doug's soul.

"O Lord, holy and true, is it time to judge those who dwell on the Earth?"[16]

The angel rose higher with sudden force, and almost as an afterthought turned to Doug.

"It's almost time," he sang before spinning in a bright blaze toward the New Jerusalem.

CHAPTER TWO

Preparations

*"Trust in the Lord with all your heart and lean not on your own understanding;
in all your ways acknowledge him, and he will make your paths straight."*

Proverbs 3:5-6

When you pick up a book on the grieving process it will more than likely quote the five stage Kubler-Ross model commonly referred to as the "grief cycle:" denial, anger, bargaining, depression, and acceptance.[1]

Although most people touch on most of the stages while processing the loss, I skipped denial and anger altogether. I had already been through those emotions four months prior to Doug's death and I knew being angry with God or denying the event in any form or fashion would do nothing for me. Questions of "why me?" or "why weren't You there?" had already been answered, my anger had already been extinguished and my questions had ceased.

Doug deployed to Iraq on November 19, 2005. Without Doug at home, I decided to travel to the states to visit family. My dog Napa stayed with a few different friends in Germany. My cat Simi stayed at home. Karen remained in Germany during the holidays and told me she would check on Simi often.

I always worried about Simi when I was gone. Simi wasn't your typical cat and I loved her dearly. I was the only human she acknowledged. On occasion she would jump into someone's lap if they had a bowl of ice cream or wore blue jeans (she was a slut for blue jeans!) but other than that, she ignored everyone but me. At night, if she wasn't curled up with me in bed, it wasn't a normal night. Simi was my shadow.

I had struggled with the decision to leave her, but it didn't make any sense to take her with me. I would have my hands full with an eleven month old who had never been on a plane before, much less an overseas flight.

Over the prior four years my faith in God had strengthened from something I believed in to something I lived. So this time, for the first time, I told God I wouldn't worry about Simi. I knew worrying was useless, and besides, God wanted me to cast my worries on Him.

"Cast all your anxiety on him because he cares for you."[2]

A few days after Christmas, Karen called. She had found Simi dead in the apartment. Simi had been fine the day prior, healthy and happy, with plenty of food and water. No one knew what had happened. Her death was unexplainable. My shock at the news was nothing like the hopelessness I felt when the soldiers knocked on my door, but it was intense. I sat on the bed and sobbed.

Then I got mad at God. I remember saying, "Why did you let this happen? I trusted you!"

If you have a beloved pet, you understand my grief. I wasn't there with her. I couldn't tell Simi how much I loved her. I couldn't reassure her. I couldn't hold her when she hurt. I couldn't do anything.

Slowly, after Simi's death, a realization gripped me with ice-cold fingertips. God was preparing me for something far, far worse.

I knew it without a doubt in my soul. God knew exactly what He was doing. He was preparing me – Doug wasn't coming home.

I queried my friends in Germany but they all dismissed me. "No, Nic," they would say. "Don't even think that."

Looking back, I know why God allowed Simi's death, and if He hadn't I don't know if my heart could have held up when those soldiers knocked on my door. Simi was a cat, a dearly loved pet, but just a cat.

The questions that came after Simi's death nagged me for months. One of my worst fears was that my cat thought I deserted her. Did she die thinking I wasn't coming home? I struggled with God for weeks. I yelled at Him, spewing out questions and quoting His biblical promises of love and protection. God met my questions with silence.

Sometimes silence from God is good. It allows you to rid yourself of pent up emotions and calm your spirit before focusing on the only One who can help. In the book of Kings the prophet Elijah had just run from an evil ruler who wanted to take his life. He was scared and exhausted when the Lord spoke to him.

The Lord said, "Go out and stand on the mountain in the presence of the Lord, for the Lord is about to pass by." Then a great and powerful wind tore the mountains apart and shattered the rocks before the Lord, but the Lord was not in the wind. After the wind there was an earthquake, but the Lord was not in the earthquake. After the earthquake came a fire, but the Lord was not in the fire. And after the fire came a gentle whisper. When Elijah heard it, he pulled his cloak over his face and went out and stood at the mouth of the cave.[3]

God wasn't in the gusting wind, the powerful earthquake, or the fire's heat; He was in a still small voice. That's why when we are internally screaming we can't hear Him. He is there, closer perhaps than He has ever been, but in His wisdom He knows that His voice would be drowned in the scream. So He waits.

After Simi's death I went back to Germany devastated and angry with God. After crying out in fury for days I found myself sitting still and listening, asking questions like "why did this happen?" And "did she know I loved her?" In a few months those questions would play a major role in my life.

After careful thought, I came to understand God created Simi. He loved her even more than I did, and although humans are made in God's image all creatures are under His watchful gaze. *"Look at the birds of the air; they do not sow or reap or store away in barns, and yet your heavenly Father feeds them. Are you not much more valuable than they?"[4]*

Although it devastated me that I wasn't there with Simi, as I read scripture I began to realize God was present despite my absence. *"Where can I go from your Spirit? Where can I flee from your presence? If I go up to the heavens, you are there; if I make my bed in the depths, you are there. If I rise on the wings of the dawn, if I settle on the far side of the sea, even there your hand will guide me, your right hand will hold me fast."[5]*

Even if my worst fears were reality and Simi didn't know how much I loved her on this Earth, she knew now because she was with my all-knowing God. All I had to do was ask God to tell Simi my heart. *"Which of you, if his son asks for bread, will give him a stone? Or if he asks for a fish, will give him a snake? If you, then, though you are evil, know how to give good gifts to your children, how much more will your Father in heaven give good gifts to those who ask him!"[6]*

All I had to do was ask. My all-powerful God, who created the heavens and the earth, had the ability to tell one beloved cat how much one of His children loved her. Peace came after that. It wasn't a peace that relieved my tears, but a peace that came with trusting God.

The questions that came after Simi's death came with a vengeance when the soldier said my name. Doug might as well have been a million miles away. I wasn't there with him. I couldn't hold him. I couldn't tell him how much I loved him. Did he know how much I loved him? Did he truly understand? Those questions came immediately, but unlike my experience earlier they ended almost instantly. God loved Doug; He was right there with him; and even if Doug didn't understand my feelings, all I had to do was talk to Daddy. God would tell Doug what I needed him to know.

Two months after Simi died and a few months before the soldiers knocked on my door, I had to give my dog away. Napa was a beautiful Siberian husky. People who didn't like dogs liked Napa. Doug and I had adopted her in Alaska, his first duty station, when we discovered her running around our neighborhood without a collar. I coaxed her into the house with a piece of caribou steak. Poor dog, thinking we would feed her steak everyday! I still laugh about that today.

But our son Dak had started crawling and he was getting on Napa's last nerve. She snapped at him, close to his eye, leaving a mark. I was startled, but told myself it would never happen again. It did. The third time the mark was unmistakable and unsettling, and for the third time it was right next to Dak's eye. I talked to Doug and told him what had happened.

Doug didn't hesitate, "Get her out of the house." Of course, I knew that is what I had to do, but I didn't want to, and I needed reassurance from Doug I was making the right decision. I should have reacted the first time Napa showed any sign of unease.

Simi was already gone. Now Napa had to go.

I gave Napa to my friends Erica and Caleb upstairs. I knew they would love her, but it hurt. My family was leaving me, one by one.

My first thought was, "Well, I can move quickly now. I don't have any pets." Again, I knew in my heart God was paving the way. Doug wasn't going to make it.

Of course, you deny those feelings. You fight them. Simi died in December; I gave Napa away in February. At that time Doug was still in Kuwait, out of the danger zone. I wished he would remain there, but he didn't. In March Doug's unit went to the epicenter of the war, Bagdad, Iraq. By May 25, 2006 I had long since buried my fears.

When I met my CAO, the Casualty Assistance Officer, one of the first questions he asked was, "Do you have any pets?" I could see the relief in his eyes when I said no. "It would be much easier," he said, "to get you back to the states without pets."

That was my next nightmare – getting back home.

The issue was, I didn't have one.

❦

As Doug walked through the gates of the New Jerusalem, his eyes lifted sky-ward, marveling as the city stretched above him as far as the eye could see. Slight variations in the structure partitioned one room from another yet blended so well at a distance you could see no distinction. Clear as crystal, the city seemed to float in the air. The gold streets below it mirrored the city's light and cast Doug in a warmth so vast he shivered.

Doorways dotted the glistening cubed city, but all of them were shut, save one. People walked by him, laughing and whispering together, but none of them made a move to enter the structure, only traverse around it on its wide, golden streets.

As if in answer to his thoughts a tall man stepped beside him, dark hair cascading down his back in glorious disarray. His frame was almost twice the size of Doug's yet he had a widening grin that was almost childlike. His dark eyes sparkled as he nodded toward the city.

"The gift of the New Jerusalem is for after the millennial reign of our Savior," he said, lips curving into a mysterious smile.

Although Doug had never met the man, he instantly knew his identity: Samson.

Doug opened his mouth to introduce himself but then thought better of it. As he perused the faces of those passing by, he realized he knew their names as if he had known them his entire life.

Samson read the realization in Doug's eyes and chuckled. "Each day will bring more surprises," he said as he slapped Doug's back. "Our Father loves surprises."

Samson pointed to the open door and motioned Doug inside, "Come, Father does let us see the center."

Doug followed Samson through the threshold, noticing the inside walls were fashioned from the same crystal clear jasper as the city itself. There were no lights, yet there was no need of illumination. The same brilliance outside reached inside as well, lighting the empty room with a beauty Doug could only wonder at.

"The city does not need the sun or the moon to shine on it, for the glory of God gives it light."[7]

Above him and to each side were more rooms. Although the walls surrounding him seemed transparent, he couldn't see past them. It was a gloriously odd feeling. Standing in the room, Doug felt completely alone with his Creator, yet passages within arms reach teemed with treasures and people. The city was unbroken fellowship and individual privacy.

"Our rooms are prepared outside the city and brought here when we fade on Earth," Samson said as he too gazed in wonder at the radiance of the place. "Just like the temple of old, no sound can invade the peace of the New Jerusalem, no tool can be used near God's dwelling place.[8] Angels bring our rooms here when they are complete. This is the last door still open on the lower level. Time is moving quickly. We will soon witness the return of the King." Samson motioned to a large window in the back. "But until this room is finished by the Carpenter for the individual who will live here, we are allowed a glimpse inside the future glory."

Doug had been so engrossed in the beauty of the bare walls he hadn't made a move to peer out the window. When he did, he let out a low whistle. Towers, rising it seemed to the height of the moon, filled his vision. Glorious new colors glistened on each, casting the center of the New Jerusalem in a rainbow bonfire. Stairwells ascending from the golden streets circled unencumbered into the air and led to the tops of each tower like sparkling spider webs. Trees and rocks and even mountains rose from the city's floor to merge with the buildings as if they were one and the same structure.

He was looking at a paradise as well as a city: Eden and the house of the Lord. And it was his home.

Sampson leaned against the crystal clear wall, face reflecting the glory of the scene just outside.

"I never grow tired of coming here," he said quietly. "When every room is finished, each resident will have a view of the city. We will surround it on all four sides. Every believer will be with everyone else, yet have their own private place to call home. Some will be attached to mountains, others to buildings. Some will have a stairwell right outside their door. Everyone will be surrounded by those they love, some old friends and some new. Although we will have unbroken fellowship with every saint, some relationships are unique and will become even more special."

Doug smiled. He and Nic would continue to grow closer here. Their insecurities and fears would no longer be present. Ambitions and selfishness would fade away. Their jobs would be together and their time undivided. Their Father would love them and Jesus would guide them. They hadn't even begun to realize the heights their relationship could achieve.

"How big is it?" Doug asked, suddenly realizing he couldn't see the end of the city. The interior walls of the New Jerusalem stretched well beyond his vision.

"Each wall is roughly fifteen hundred miles wide and tall.[9] Billions of people can live here without any lack of privacy or any want of companionship. That is, when they choose to tarry here."

"What do you mean?" Doug asked, surprised. "I thought this would be our home."

Samson laughed. "You don't think we will be in these rooms for eternity do you? No, there is an entire world to explore, even new worlds to explore.[10] In eternity Father will allow us full access to His creation. But this," Samson said as he lifted his arms and motioned to the window, "this will always be home."

Doug looked up at the sky as if he could see the stars. God's glory was so encompassing no other light could penetrate this place. Yet, Doug could sense God's creation still out there, teeming with brilliance. Was Samson talking about the stars? Galaxies? Would they explore everything God had made?

When Doug glanced back at the warrior, Samson had a huge grin on his face. "I thought the same when I first arrived here. The stars? But why not?" he said, laughing. "Father knows we want to see them; He gave us that desire. After the millennial reign of our Savior, when everyone has chosen the Son as King, well, we will do a little traveling."

Samson released a huge belly laugh when he saw Doug's mystified expression. "Father has much in store for us, my friend. This is only the beginning."

The warrior leaned out the window and pointed to an area near the top of the New Jerusalem. "There is one area there, about three rooms from the top, ten over from the left. It is hazy to me, like a fog encompasses it. Do you see something similar?"

Doug leaned past Sampson's massive frame and looked where the warrior pointed. "Yes, I see it, but the fog is at the eleventh room over, not the tenth."

Samson grinned, still gazing longingly at the shrouded room near the top. "Tenth for me, eleventh for you. My room is the one I cannot see, yours is right beside mine, where your vision is veiled. Father put us close together. We will become good friends. Perhaps we can explore the stars together."

Before Doug could reply, Samson's countenance grew serious. He crossed his arms and furrowed his brows, examining Doug as if he were some unknown insect their Father had allowed inside the gates.

Sampson heaved an unsteady breath and nodded. "You're a man of honor. From your youth you lived righteously. I have wanted to meet you for some time. From my youth I rebelled, acting on what I desired and not what God desired for me. God used me despite my weakness, and by His grace I realized my folly. But only in the end." Samson paused, examining Doug again. "Nic just reread my story, tragic as it was, and she asked God why He would have put my story in His good book, or why, I should say, He chose me to carry out His tasks. My story is so painfully calamitous she could barely read it."[11]

Samson paused, shaking his head and chuckling under his breath. "God taught Nic something, Doug. He taught her that no matter what, if God calls you He will use you despite your faults and your fears. He will use you even if you leave His path."

Doug nodded as Nic's fear beat inside his chest. "She fears disappointing God. She fears making the wrong decisions."

Samson nodded gravely, "And the enemy will use that."

"But the enemy will fail."

Samson turned, grin widening in agreement. "Yes, he will! Father always gives victory to His children of faith. I have a surprise for you, my friend. It's something Jesus wants you to see. Something your death caused. It's happening now." Samson spun and bolted out of the empty room, muscles rippling under God's unending light, a deep resonating laughter trailing in his wake, urging Doug to follow.

CHAPTER THREE

Questions

"God will always give what is right to his people who cry to him night and day, and he will not be slow to answer them."

Luke 18:7 NCV

When death strikes, people tell you to wait a year before you make any major decisions. I think the idea of a year's wait may be an acceptable milestone if you were in your own country, in your own city, in your own house, near your parents, and surrounded by the things you love.

As a military wife overseas, I had none of those things. One of the first questions asked was, "When do you want to leave Germany?"

Leave? My life had just been turned upside down. My friends were in Germany, my life was in Germany, and my belongings were in Germany. The last time I had seen Doug was in Germany.

I blinked back tears. "I can't stay here?"

"You can stay for up to a year," Jeff, my CAO said, "but I wouldn't recommend it. To tell you the truth, the support for you is better in the states. I wouldn't recommend staying here." He said it again, making his point. I had just met Jeff but I instantly trusted him. He actually reminded me of Doug – he cared. Each time he came to see me he would sit down and say, "This is hard on me too."

I could see the pain in his eyes so I knew he spoke the truth. One of his own hadn't come home. He had a sense of duty, like Doug. I discovered later that he had volunteered for the position of CAO. He wanted to assure himself if something happened over Memorial Day weekend the survivor would be in good hands. Thanks to him, I was.

I didn't decide to return to the states for a few days, but when I did, Jeff, my friends, and my parents jumped into high gear, each relieved that I had made, in their minds, the right decision.

Then came the next question I couldn't answer. "Where do you want to go?"

My mother had moved from my hometown of Knoxville to Chattanooga, Tennessee and had recently gotten remarried. My dad was in Huntsville, Alabama, Doug's father lived in Charleston, South Carolina, and Doug's mom and step-father still resided in Doug's hometown of Plymouth, New Hampshire. I had never lived any of those places, and like most military families, my friends were scattered across the county. I knew both mine and Doug's parents would take me in; even my friends would have thrown out their guest room furniture and offered me a place indefinitely. But what did I want?

The only fact I knew with certainty was that I needed to be alone. I didn't want to have to put on a false front of strength when I needed to break down; and I needed to talk to God. I knew He had the answers and I knew I needed to listen.

I also knew there would be a service held for Doug in Plymouth, New Hampshire. My first stop had to be there.

Then I thought of Doug's grandmother's house. It was sitting vacant in Doug's hometown of Plymouth after a recent fall had placed her in a nursing home. At the time her move had devastated the family. Less than a month later it was a huge blessing for me.

Over the course of days, the answer came. I would go to Plymouth and stay at Gram's house until I could figure things out.

But the question still bothered me. Where would I ultimately live? I literally could have taken a map of the United States and thrown a dart at it to pick a place. I am a planner by nature, and it frustrated me that I didn't have a plan. So I began formulating one. I would move to Grams and then drive south, visiting the places I thought I may want to settle. Ironically, Doug and I had done a "where do you want to retire" trip before we left for Germany. I could backtrack to the places we liked and visit family and friends along the way. Whatever felt right, well, that is where I would stay.

With my decision made I felt better, and Tara, God bless her, said she would accompany me on the trip. A great burden lifted off my shoulders when Tara said she would come to the states. Tara and I had grown extremely close since our husbands' deployment. We didn't want to say goodbye.

I know that is why she volunteered and I know that is why I felt such relief when she did.

I was terrified to leave the friends that had inundated me with love ever since those soldiers knocked on my door.

Tara was always there beside me, arriving when I woke and leaving only when I went to bed. Jessica and Jan were my defenders, shielding me from planning anything on my own. Rachelle was my light, my faithful shield of protection. And then there was Monica and Erica, Kristine and Paige, Kim and Karen, and Joanna and Erin. They aren't just forever family, they are blood.

I felt like I was saying goodbye to everything I had ever known. I was leaving friends who understood, not one, but twelve. My things would be packed and shipped across the ocean. It would take months for my belongings to reach the states and then weeks for the shipment to arrive wherever I decided to live. My car wouldn't arrive for months. My things, Doug's clothes, our memories, I had to leave behind. Once I boarded that plane, my life, as I knew it, was no more.

It was a crippling feeling. My husband was gone, my pets were gone, and my friends, really my family, waved goodbye.

I stepped on the plane with my mom, Dak, and an assisting officer, with no home and no place to call home, crawled into my seat, and cried.

❧

Doug could feel Nic's confusion. Its beat echoed in his chest and sent an ache inside his spirit. Although there were moments he could barely comprehend the cost of his death, he knew he was where he was supposed to be.

He stopped well past the city walls, in a large field dotted with small, white flowers that emitted a fragrance more beautiful than the finest perfume.

Doug turned to look at the retreating figure of his new friend. Samson's large frame bounded over the lush ground toward the city of God. As Doug turned back to the object of his interest, more and more angels glided past, like shooting stars in the bright of day, each surging effortlessly toward the New Jerusalem.

In the short time he had been in Heaven the pace had accelerated. The end was near. Jesus' return to Earth was approaching faster than those left behind could fathom.

The anticipation of seeing his family again sent rivers of delight to his soul yet he knew some of them would choose to deny the name of God. It was a strange sensation, yet now that he was with God, to deny Him was to renounce everything good. It was like throwing out all the presents on Christmas morning in full view of those who had given them.

Life was a choice. Choosing God was the greatest choice you could make. It was the choice everyone born should make. Yet it was a choice many pushed aside.

The Word even states that those who deny God can offer no apologies. *"For since the creation of the world God's invisible qualities — his eternal power and divine nature — have been clearly seen, being understood from what has been made, so that men are without excuse."*[1]

His thoughts turned back to Nic. She was at a crossroads, but in time she would follow the road God had laid out for her. Doug picked up one of the stones at his feet and ran his fingers over its flawless surface. In Heaven, instead of bricks, there were diamonds, rubies, jaspers, and emeralds. Instead of cement, there was silver and gold. Doug turned to survey the buildings surrounding him, shimmering like prisms in the glorious light.

Lifting his eyes skyward, the angel building the wall before him glistened against the flawless backdrop of diamonds. The angel's wings moved so quickly Doug saw only a residue of their flight. He heard their movement deep inside his soul as if a hummingbird lived within his chest. It was the most glorious sound he had ever heard. Even if he sat here for days, he would never grow tired of watching the diamonds appear below his feet or see the angel's skill in laying them.

Rewards. They were often ignored on Earth. Churches never preached about the rewards God offered His children, but rewards were real.

"Behold, I am coming soon! My reward is with me, and I will give to everyone according to what he has done."[2]

Yes, rewards were real. Doug watched as the angel laid the next stone in place. A refreshing breeze glided past, bringing with it the call of an eagle and the echo of other workers, building other heavenly homes. But this home was special.

This one was Nic's.

Although Nic didn't feel like she had a home on Earth, she wasn't supposed to. There was a purpose behind his death, a purpose that in time Nic would realize. God wanted her to look up, focus her sights on His coming kingdom, and tell others. Nic would soon realize her focus wasn't on the life she had lost, but on the one God was saving for her when Jesus was crowned King.

Doug could barely wait for Nic to see this place. He could almost see her eyes widen in delightful surprise and hear her embarrassed laugh as the Son of Man presented her with a house far more glorious than anything anyone deserved.

Samson had told him he could see the construction process for those still alive. The angels worked on houses here and transported them to the city at the moment of death. His had been completed the second the IED took his life. When the angels carried him to Jesus, his room had been taken to the New Jerusalem. After the millennial reign of Christ, God the Father would descend to the Earth with the city and live among believers. The angels would sing, "Now the dwelling of God is with men, and he will live with them. They will be his people, and God himself will be with them and be their God. He will wipe every tear from their eyes. There will be no more death or mourning or crying or pain, for the old order of things has passed away."[3]

But that was after the millennial reign of his Savior. First, Jesus would descend with all the saints and usher in a thousand years of peace. All believers would have the privilege of living on a renewed Earth for a millennium with a perfect King before the old order of things passed away.

Doug chuckled as he thought of the houses he and Nic had lived in over the years, the first being a temporary two room basement apartment in Alaska as they searched for a place to stay. That is where he had taken Nic after their wedding. They had moved six times in six years in the Army, and Nic would have to move a few more times in the coming months.

Doug stepped closer, drawn to the glittering structure as if he had helped form it. He smiled as he realized that he, in fact, had. As he ran his hand over the smooth stones he saw their differences. The ones at the foundation were opaque, with a silverfish tint. Those were the stones that had been fashioned in Nic's early years of belief, when her vision was somewhat influenced by her teachers and the books she read. The ones the angel was now placing, the flawless transparent diamonds, came after his death, when Nic started reading the scriptures for herself, calling on God's Spirit to reveal what He wanted her to discover. Those stones were fashioned by faith and faith alone, trusting in God and the hope of His coming.

Doug's hand hit something. He moved back, surprised to find a tiny rose growing between the opaque stones and the flawless diamonds. It was no bigger than his fingernail, but so vividly red he was shocked that he hadn't noticed it before. Although any other observer might think it was a battle wound against unmarred crystal, the rose's unique beauty only magnified the stones surrounding it.

Another diamond appeared at his feet. Doug smiled and picked it up. The angel could barely keep up the pace.

Nic was crying again, but with those tears came words of faith and that faith was rewarded.

Doug moved the stone toward the rose. God's unending light caused the rose to be reflected in its surface.

"God can make beauty out of pain, Nic," Doug said as he turned the stone and watched the crimson reflection sparkle under God's unending light. "Hurry up, Jesus. I can't wait to see my Nic again."

~

Before I left Germany, the military had a service to honor Doug and another soldier killed in the blast, Specialist Robert Blair.

That morning I met with my CAO. I knew in a few hours I would be attending the services. I was terrified, tired, and fearful of the experience.

If you have ever been to a military service, you will understand my trepidation. They place boots, a helmet, and a gun in front, representing the missing soldier. At the end of the service they do a roll call. They say a few soldiers' names who are present and the soldiers' respond with a "Here, sir." Then they call out the name of the missing service member. In my case, it went something like this.

"Captain DiCenzo."

Silence.

"Captain Doug DiCenzo."

Silence.

"Captain Douglas DiCenzo."

And then the guns sound off, honoring the fallen soldier.

If that won't rip your heart from your chest, nothing will.

My CAO knew I was dreading the experience. Although Jeff was an outstanding soldier, he was also an understanding man.

"Do you trust me?" Jeff asked.

I stared at him. Did I trust him? What kind of a question was that?

He placed a piece of paper on the table. "I need you to sign this. I have already reviewed it with your parents. They agree with me; you don't need to know about this right now. Sign it, and I will tell you about it later."

I signed the paper.

When the time of the service arrived, I was escorted into the church I had fought hard to reserve for the funeral. The services were supposed to be held in the movie theater on post. It was neutral ground and was considered "Standard Operating Procedure" for military services in Baumholder. I couldn't visualize Doug's services being held there. Doug and I were Christians and the movie theater was a run-down, impersonal building.

Surprisingly, the military fought me for days. It seems I was the first person who challenged their view of what a military funeral service should look like. Jessica and Jan talked to those in charge, making the point that what I was requesting was not unreasonable or unsound. They heard time and again it wasn't "Standard Operating Procedure."

I didn't give up the fight and in the end the military agreed to hold the services in the chapel.

I had also requested a picture of Doug and Dak be placed beside the boots, rifle, and gun. Although it was a military service, I wanted the people in the chapel to see Doug for the man he was, not just a soldier in uniform. As I stated previously, those in charge could barely agree to hold the services in the church, so when I requested the picture it sent them into a tailspin. They told Jessica and Jan time and again, "That isn't the way we do things." The fight went on for days, but in the end my request was granted.

So when I was ushered into the church, passing hoards of those gathered to pay their respects for not only Doug, but also for Specialist Robert Blair, there was a picture of Doug holding Dak next to the empty boots. Beside Blair's gear stood a picture of him in a cowboy hat at a rodeo. During the service, the speaker told stories of Blair participating in rodeos with a passion for life. I didn't know Robert Blair at all before the service, but I knew him instantly when I saw that picture and heard those stories. It was Blair as he was, not just a soldier in uniform. It was Blair. I heard the same comments about Doug. If you didn't know Doug when you entered the church you knew him when you left.

That picture of Doug and Dak helped me get through the service because it was my husband they were honoring, not just a soldier. A soldier had died, but so had a husband and a father. I thank the military for allowing that picture, and I hope they do so again if another spouse so requests.

The guns went off. I was clinging to Jeff's hand so hard I probably drew blood. No matter how much you expect it, it not only scares you, it stops your heart. It is final. It is the end.

After the guns sounded I ran out of the church as fast as I possibly could.

When I was safely in the car, Jeff leaned against the door.

"Do you remember that paper you signed today?"

I knew whatever Jeff had to say would be devastating. I reached for the hand of the person beside me. Honesty, I don't remember whose hand it was.

Jeff proceeded to tell me Doug's remains were being flown to Plymouth for the services there, but if any more remains were found the army would notify me.

I had signed a piece of paper stating if any more of my husband was found I would want to know.

I was frantic. The day after the soldiers came to my door I was told my Doug had been hit by an IED while traveling in his vehicle. He wasn't pronounced dead until forty minutes after being airlifted away. I thought he had suffered. My worst fear was that he had suffered. Jeff reassured me the report said "killed instantly." I asked about the time difference. Jeff said he would check into it.

Jeff came back the next day and restated that Doug was killed instantly, but because there wasn't a licensed doctor on the scene they had to wait until he arrived at the hospital to pronounce him legally dead.

But I had signed a form stating they may be looking for more of his remains. Jeff assured me this was normal procedure, but the scenario it presented was a scenario I hadn't allowed my mind to contemplate. Was all of him there?

I don't remember the drive back to the apartment or what else happened that night. My mind was awash with questions and fears. I do know it was my final night in Germany. My things had been packed and I was staying with Tara. Jessica and Jan lingered at Tara's after everyone else had gone. None of us wanted to say goodbye. When they finally left I turned to Tara and sobbed, "Was his head there?"

I don't know why that particular image bothered me. I think when something tragic happens you have visions of your loved one's face, staring blankly ahead, pain etched in the corner of their eyes. Doug had such a happy face; my vision of it in pain and lifeless terrified me. What terrified me even more was if his head was missing.

I sobbed so loudly that Jessica and Jan burst back into the room. Tara was already holding me, and then all three of them were. That was the first time, I believe, I truly broke down. Now I understand why each thread of the World Trade Center was combed with a microscope. You want your entire loved one, every last molecule.

They brought the first urn to me in Plymouth, a few days before the services there. One month later I received a call from my new CAO in the states. They had found more of Doug. The second urn would be flown in that next week.

The questions were coming faster than I would have liked. Now the scenario in my mind was an actuality. Some of Doug hadn't been attached to his body.

The visions you have are absolutely horrific. Every scenario possible plays out in your mind. I started asking questions. *What came home first? And what was in the second urn?*

I suppose many people wouldn't want to know, but I had to. My plans at the time were to scatter some of Doug's ashes and keep some until I died and then we could be buried and/or scattered together. I needed to know what to do with urn number one and urn number two.

I said to Bob, my stateside CAO, "His hands need to stay with me, but his feet need to be on the mountaintop."

Bob replied with, "Then you need to keep urn number two."

His reply indicated he knew more than he wanted to reveal. Quite understandably, the army tries to shield a spouse from any further pain, but at times knowledge is better than ignorance. I needed to know the truth, and if a wife needs to know the truth she isn't going to stop until she finds it.

As the Bible says, *"Love is as strong as death, its jealousy unyielding as the grave. It burns like blazing fire, like a mighty flame. Many waters cannot quench love; rivers cannot wash it away."*[4]

The truth came over five months later, but not until after I received urn number three.

ᘀᓇ

Doug knew Nic was about to receive the phone call. He ran up the mountain with his bare feet, toes curling in the soft verdant grass.

His breath came quickly, but without weariness. His muscles burned, but without any pain. The air was thick with oxygen and the wind against his face was slightly cool, yet warm enough to keep his body limber.

The soft pad of his footsteps echoed in his head. The stones he brushed didn't tear his skin; on the contrary, they seemed to thrust him onward, upward, and further along the path.

God's unceasing light darted down through the branches, running with him. The trees were enormous, their bark rich with life. The leaves shivered as he passed, urging him faster.

There was no sweat, no ache, no nausea, not even a thought of rest.

He had never been more alive.

He broke out of the tree line, laughing as the wind picked up and the stones beneath his feet grew larger, sparkling under Gods ever-present light, singing with him.

It wasn't long until he was bounding over boulders, almost flying, soaring farther than he ever had before. His muscles strained, but there was never a moment he thought he wouldn't land on his feet or reach his destination. His toes gripped the stone as if he had the paws of a mountain lion.

Faster he went.

Nic was getting the phone call now.

Doug pushed harder, knowing he had to reach the top. He had to be there to tell her. He had to tell her. . .

The crest of the mountain came into focus; his breath came faster; he pushed harder.

Then he was running on level ground, dancing in the mountain meadow, red and yellow wildflowers swaying as he turned full circle with arms wide. His words were thunder, his voice engulfed the surging waters of the raging river far below.

"I'm alive, Nic! Believe it. Know it. I'm alive!"

ᑲᓕ

It was six months and five days after Doug's death when I received the phone call.

"Nic, are you sitting down?" Bob, my stateside CAO, said.

I knew as soon as he spoke those words what he had called to tell me. As I listened to Bob's words my body just went numb, and unlike when the soldiers knocked on my door the tears gushed forth without any hesitation. I remember my frantic voice asking Bob why it had taken six months to identify more of my husband and what part of Doug was arriving in urn number three.

Bob tried to steer me away from those questions. "Nic," he said gently, as he had done so many times before, "the army knows how important it is to identify every piece of your loved one. If they find a hair, a shard of fingernail, they conduct a DNA test to see if it matches that of your loved one."

I understood what he was saying, but unbeknownst to him, I had opened urn number one and urn number two. I had held the bags of ash in my hands. I knew urn number two wasn't a fragment of hair. It was much more substantial. What had happened to my Doug? What was coming? And what else was out there?

I don't think any words can do my emotions justice. All I can say is with each urn you relive everything you have already been through, and with each memory the wounds not only double, they multiply.

The questions were coming more rapidly now. What did my Doug look like when they pulled him from the vehicle? Did he feel the blast? Did he suffer? What was in urn number three?

The day the army delivered the third urn I was still at Gram's house in Plymouth and my gracious God had allowed one of my closest friends to be there. Rachelle had come from Germany to spend a month with her parents while her husband Scott was deployed. One of her first stops was to see me. If anyone in this world has the faith I have, it is Rachelle. I knew Rachelle would support me in what I had to do.

When Bob handed me urn number three, I told him to wait as I flipped it over, took a screwdriver from my pocket, and started unscrewing the bottom plate holding the wooden box together. I had asked and the army wasn't answering. I had requested and the army was dodging my questions. What was the state of my husband when they found his body? How much of Doug would I find in urn number three?

I think Bob may have had a heart attack in the kitchen of Gram's house. He turned white as a sheet.

I hesitated, but only for a second. Bob was a good man, a gentle man, the kind of man who would want to protect me at all cost, but he didn't understand how much I needed to know what had happened on May 25, 2006. What was in urn number three?

As the screws to the urn fell on the table, I think Bob realized how much this wife needed to know just what had happened to her husband.

As I drew the ash out of the urn, I knew instantly it wasn't just a piece of hair.

After that day, Bob called to tell me what he knew. Although I still didn't know what Doug looked like, I only knew of "torso" and "skin particles" and "ribs," I did know there was much more to the story. I discovered what that story was a few weeks later when Jessica and her husband Grant came to visit.

Grant was one of Doug's platoon leaders, and although Grant hadn't been there when the IED ripped Doug apart, he had arrived on the scene fifteen minutes later. He was there when they pulled Doug from the vehicle. Grant would tell me what I needed to know.

∽

When Grant and Jessica arrived, I was thrilled to have them. I didn't know Grant well, but I liked him, and Jessica and I had grown close in Germany when our husbands deployed.

I had first met Jess when Doug was introduced to the company during a Family Readiness Meeting. The FRG (Family Readiness Group) is established so when soldiers deploy there is a system in place to communicate to the wives what, if anything, the unit can tell them about their husbands downrange. Because Doug was the commander of the unit, I led the group, and Jessica volunteered to be my co-leader. We relayed information from the unit back to the spouses. We distributed information, organized meals, helped resolve issues, and steered them to the right organizations.

Jess immediately took charge of the FRG on May 25, 2006 and became my cherished defender. Since then we have formed a bond that is impenetrable.

When Grant arrived he asked when I wanted to talk. I said the sooner the better. When Dak went down for a nap, Grant relayed what he had seen.

Doug was in the passenger side of the vehicle when the IED detonated right beside his door. The force of the explosion ripped through Doug's door and body armor. It was the most powerful explosion Grant had ever seen. The roof had even been blown off the vehicle.

Doug had been severed at his waist. Everything below that line was in tact; everything above that line was destroyed so completely not much of Doug was recognizable.

One of Doug's soldiers found his arm, another a piece of his nose. The rest of Doug they recovered was a mess of tissue and skin fragments. One of the men walking from the site had blood covering him, but it wasn't his own. It was Doug's.

Why three urns? Now I had my answer.

In a way, my vision of Doug's death was worse than the truth. Although I didn't imagine anything so gruesome, I now knew Doug felt no pain. As Grant said, "One moment he was with us, the next he was with the Lord."

I also discovered something else, something beautiful. With the information I now had, I realized how many miracles occurred that day in hell, when the IED exploded and my husband met Jesus. God was taking care of me in that heartbeat of a second. My God knew what I needed and He made sure I received it.

CHAPTER FOUR
Messages from Hell

"The righteous perish, and no one ponders it in his heart; devout men are taken away, and no one understands that the righteous are taken away to be spared from evil. Those who walk uprightly enter into peace; they find rest as they lie in death."

Isaiah 57:1-2

When I first heard the news one of my first questions was, "Can you send me his wedding ring?"

Doug had proposed less than four months after our first date, just before he entered ranger school, an intense army-training course that can last at the minimum two months. During that time most contact to the outside world comes to a grinding halt. Letters are the only form of communication between grueling weeks of training. Phone calls last minutes once every three weeks.

It was a hard time, yet during those weeks of Doug's absence, I was busy packing up my house and saying goodbye to my friends. Our plan was for me to meet him after he graduated ranger school and take a cross-country drive to Alaska, his first duty station.

When we arrived in Alaska, we rented a room at a bed and breakfast, found a justice of the peace, and got married outside the morning after the first snowfall. If I had to do it over again I wouldn't change a thing. There was no family, no rehearsal dinner, no budget, no stress or burdens, just Doug and myself, the fresh snow, and a weekend alone. At that time I had engraved inside his wedding ring, "ILU always."

Nine months later we had another wedding, this one for family and friends in New Hampshire. For this wedding I added "& forever" to the inside of his ring.

A few days before I left Germany the ring arrived from Iraq. The army officials gave it to Jessica and Jan to give to me. When my friends examined it they became concerned about my reaction.

They warned me cautiously, "Nic, this went through an explosion and then they had to pry it off his hand. It is warped."

I assured them I didn't care; but when they drew the ring from the envelope my heart skipped a beat. At this time I didn't know how horrific the explosion was, and I didn't know that his left hand wasn't even attached to his body. In fact, years later I discovered they almost didn't find his hand. It had gotten wedged below his seat and wasn't discovered until days after the explosion.

If Doug's hand hadn't been sheltered under that seat, they may have never found the ring. Grant also said the vehicle was twisted metal and melted steel. Debris of all sorts was strewn throughout the streets of Bagdad. The ring could have been lost in the trenches of Iraq or the twisted metal that remained.

The ring is now oblong, like an ellipse, and one side of that ellipse has cascaded in slightly. I am a petite person, weighing just over a hundred pounds. Doug wasn't a large man or a tall man, but his fingers were twice the size of mine. Now his ring fits perfectly on my thumb, as if God himself had directed the impact so I could wear Doug's ring without fearing it would slip off.

The ring wasn't the only thing the men sent back from Iraq. Jess and Jan also handed me Doug's dog tags. On them was something I was unprepared to see. It was a key engraved with, "I love you."

Of course, I was the one who had given Doug the key, but I hadn't seen it in years. I had two keys engraved for Doug before he entered ranger school and had given the keys to him on the eve before he left. Soldiers could put one additional item on their dog tags and I had hoped Doug would wear a key to remind him of me.

I don't remember where I bought them. They looked like they were made for a set of luggage, small enough for Doug to carry easily but symbolic enough to be appropriate. I still remember the engraver looking at the keys and commenting, "These are very thin. They may break under the stress of the engraving." But they didn't. The engraver handed them back to me slightly surprised that the "I love you" message was intact. When I handed them to Doug, I also gave him a typed note that read:

I love you
Be careful out there
I will be thinking about you
Always
And if there is ever a bad time
Look at the key
And remember
That is what I am thinking
At the moment.

Doug sent me a letter a few weeks after entering ranger school - the first key had been lost.

After that day, I recall seeing the second key only once during our first year of marriage. I never saw it again. When Doug was killed we had been married just shy of six years. I had assumed both keys had been lost. They were flimsy, cheap metal. They shouldn't have stood up to any strain at all, much less an explosion.

Doug's dog tags were discovered dangling on a knob in front of his body. Now how is that possible? Doug's body armor was gone; his upper body was gone; yet the dog tags, looking brand new, were hanging on a knob. Did Daddy's hand take those dog tags and place them there? That sounds like my Daddy. God knows what you need to keep you holding on one more day. I look at the wedding ring and the key as a miracle. Although I lost the most important thing in my life, God made sure I had what I needed to hold on.

I knew as soon as I saw the key the message was no longer a message from me to Doug, but from Doug to me.

"I love you. Be careful out there. I will be thinking about you – always. And if there is ever a bad time look at the key and remember that is what I am thinking at the moment."

When I glance at the dog tags and the key I think about that message. I wear the ring daily and I see the key daily. What I didn't expect was to have messages continue to come, messages only God could send, messages even more precious than these.

❧

Doug slowly lowered his hands, wondering, hoping, and praying Nic had heard him.

"I'm alive," he whispered. He closed his eyes and let God's light warm his face, shivering as his breath eased and his muscles relaxed.

The wildflowers danced with anticipation and the river below roared with God's renewing strength.

This was not the end.

Everything in this place whispered those words, quivered with excitement and betrayed the beauty of the coming of the Lamb.

"Behold I am coming soon!"[1]

Doug hadn't realized how close Jesus' second coming was while he was on Earth, but Nic had. After September 11, 2001, Nic had started researching biblical prophecy. She had been fascinated by the end times as a young girl and that fire had come rushing back after she saw the second plane hit the Twin Towers.

A small smile crept across Doug's face as he remembered Nic sitting in their Alaskan home reading aloud opposing views of Revelation as he made pancakes. Biblical prophecy wasn't quite what he wanted to hear on his day off, but that's when he wasn't a true believer. By the world's standards he was a good man, a model American, a loving husband, and an exemplary moral leader, but that fell far short in God's eyes. He was a sinner, like everyone else. No matter how good you were by the world's standards, it wasn't enough.

"We all, like sheep, have gone astray, each of us has turned to his own way; and the Lord has laid on him the iniquity of us all."[2]

But that had changed. When he delved deeper into the Word he saw the truth. Now, when God saw him, God the Father saw God the Son.

"For all of you who were baptized into Christ have clothed yourselves with Christ."[3]

It was a biblical promise. When you believed in the Word made flesh, you became a new creation.

"Therefore, if anyone is in Christ, he is a new creation; the old has gone, the new has come!"[4]

When he fully believed he wore the garment of his Savior – spotless, sinless, without fault or stain. Then there was a shift in his focus, a hunger to know the One who knitted him together at birth, a yearning to understand the One who gave His blood to save him from an eternity of darkness.[5]

Once he believed the truth, the truth began oozing from his pores in ways he wouldn't have thought possible. Slight words he might have said flippantly he caught on the tip of his tongue, actions that would have seemed innocent became suspect, feelings he allowed to muster in his soul became increasingly unwelcome.

Jesus was transforming Nic too, slowly, step by step into a person even more beautiful than the one he had married. When Jesus returned, Nic would be perfected.

A sudden cry on the ram's horn riveted him to attention. Shouts from the redeemed echoed across the valley. In the distance, the New Jerusalem sparked midst the lush vegetation as if the stars themselves had come to rest upon the face of Heaven.

Bright shots of light exploded skyward from all around him, thousands and thousands of them, soaring toward the New Jerusalem like eternal fireworks.

The angels' light spun to the skies, twirling and spinning God's glory as they sang, "Salvation belongs to our God, who sits on the throne, and to the Lamb!"[6]

The preparations had begun.

Doug spun as excitement bubbled inside him. He quickly found the path down the mountain as a longing to return to the city of God enveloped him. The pull of God's presence was like water for the parched, food for the starving. The force of God's call intensified with each step he took.

Sudden laughter burst from him, competing with the voices of the angels, echoing over the boulders, increasing his excitement even more. But before he could start his decent, before his feet could touch the path, his Father's voice stopped him in his tracks, warming his spirit like a fire, yet sending with that fire a soft, yet firm command.

"My child," God said, "Your request has been granted. I will open the door."

CHAPTER FIVE

Messages From Heaven

And now these three remain: faith, hope and love. But the greatest of these is love.

1 Cor 13:13

Rachelle stopped in mid-stride, unable to take her eyes off the man jogging toward her. He was at the end of the hospital corridor so she couldn't make out his face, but she knew that casual yet determined gait. It couldn't be. Shaking her head, she blinked as a tall, thin doctor bumped into her.

"Excuse me," the doctor said under his breath as he hastened down the hall, obscuring the distant figure from view.

Rachelle slowly began to put one foot in front of the other, but her eyes remained focused. Something in her mind told her she hadn't been mistaken. She felt the small, still voice in her spirit urging her to pay attention.

The doctor turned, clearing her view of the corridor. The man she thought she would never see again was still there, and although his steps had slowed, his urgency remained. She shivered, but not from the cold.

Doug was dead. He had been killed instantly when an IED penetrated his body armor. Rachelle waited as Doug approached, smiling in that easy-go-lucky manner of his. He seemed to be more confident, more sure. Rachelle studied his face, searching for answers.

He nodded in greeting as he stopped before her, shifting his weight from side to side as if he was just pausing to say hello before continuing his morning run.

Rachelle had gone numb. He was dead, wasn't he? But as she studied Doug's face she could see every pore, every crevice, and every slight variation of skin tone. Rachelle had never seen him more alive.

Yes, Doug was dead. She could see that truth reflected in his light brown eyes, dotted with the smallest flecks of green. His smile widened, as if he had just let her in on a joke.

"I'm dreaming," she said.

He nodded slightly, almost fatherly, and waited for her to understand the implications of his appearance.

The still, small voice in her spirit rose like a tidal wave, entreating her to focus. This was no ordinary dream. This was a dream from God.

Rachelle drew a deep breath, telling her spirit to calm. She and Nic were close, causing a sudden urge to reach out and pull Doug toward her, force him out of the dream and into the world that had taken him.

The chill Rachelle had felt when she first saw Doug came rushing back. Although this was a dream, Doug himself was standing before her.

Doug's smile deepened when he saw her realization. Then, as if hearing a distant call, his eyes flickered beyond her, peering through her dream into an entirely different dimension. His face seemed to shimmer and for a moment his urgency returned. His eyes darted back to her with a confidence that was almost frightening.

"I need you to tell Nic something for me," he said, pausing to make sure she was listening. "I need you to tell her I love her and I want to be with her."

Rachelle's excitement built. "You can tell her yourself. She's right down that hall!" she said, pointing down the corridor where the doctor had disappeared. "She's here, in the hospital. She's. . . " Rachelle caught herself. Nic was in the hospital in her dream, not in actuality. The hospital only symbolized Nic's suffering.

Her eyes locked on Doug's. "Please, can you — "

For the first time, Doug lost his smile. "I can't, Rachelle. You have to tell her for me. Will you tell her for me? I love her and I want to be with her. Can you tell her that?"

Sudden understanding spurred Rachelle's gut. Nic was in too much pain to hear anything right now. She needed someone else to tell her, someone she trusted.

"I will."

Doug's smiled reappeared before he moved forward. Then he was gone. As quickly as he had come, Doug was gone. Rachelle was left standing in the corridor, nurses trudging by her, wondering whether or not Nic would believe what she had to tell her.

༄

Doug continued his flight down the mountain. Rachelle would deliver his message now. Doug had voiced his concern when he was on his knees before Jesus, thanking him for his life, and for Nic. He had meant to write Nic a letter from Iraq, just in case the worst happened, but he had never found the time or the strength to do so. Doug knew his request pushed the limits, but as he was on his knees in front of his Savior, looking at nail-scarred feet, he had a thought. Although it was a radical request, his God was a radical God. A God who would become human by choice? A God who would choose to suffer and die for a fallen world? A God who loved so thoroughly He wouldn't accept eternity without His fallen creation? If anyone was radical, it was Jesus. Doug took a chance. Jesus had smiled and said, "Love is stronger than death."

Doug grinned. Nic would understand the perpetuality of his message in time, and once she did she would cling to his words and not let go. The call of the ram's horn came again and with it an exhilarating shout from the angels, causing the trees Doug passed to billow despite the calmness in the air. Their leaves rustled in time with the angels' voices. Doug's heart surged with joy as he realized what he was about to witness.

He could hear the angels' continued song: "Salvation belongs to our God, who sits on the throne, and to the Lamb!"[1]

His vision was sharper, almost humorously so. He could see every slight vein in the leaves, every small indention in the rock. And his hearing . . .

Even the birds' song was clearer here. As he darted down the path, Doug could even understand the meaning behind their music. They sang of life and love and reunion. They sang of the coming of the Lamb. Although there was no breeze, the air surrounding him was moving faster, like a molecular explosion.

Doug thought back to his message as God's invisible call urged him forward, closer to the New Jerusalem. Doug hoped Nic knew he missed her, but it wasn't in the earthy way; it was with eager anticipation.

"Nic, He's coming. You know it. Believe it. Jesus is on His way." Doug smiled as a distant movement caught his eye. A pack of snow leopards were bounding down the mountain with him, leaping and dancing over the rocky path, mysteriously drawn to the presence of God. The soft pad of their feet matched his own stride. Their eyes didn't flicker his way, all of their concentration riveted on the goal – the New Jerusalem. Light filtered through tree canopy overhead, causing the leopards' hide to glisten silver.

Overhead, a hawk's song ricocheted off the boulders as it surged toward God's city. A stream in the distance roared with anticipation of the coming of the Lamb.

Doug was soon moving among the leopards, bounding down the path with them. Doug reached out and fingered their soft fur, and then they were past him, moving more quickly than he, closer to the commanding cry of the ram's horn, closer to their Maker.

He could sense Nic's unease. She knew Heaven existed. But no one knew what eternity would bring: what would it look like, taste like, be like? Would they be together? That was her biggest fear. He had only lived thirty years on Earth, and he and Nic had only been married five of those years. Nic now saw her life as an eternity, but it was really just a blink of an eye.

A verse in Mark 12:25 haunted her. It read, *"When the dead rise, they will neither marry nor be given in marriage; they will be like the angels in heaven."* He had been taken away too soon, Nic thought. She wanted to be with him and she didn't know if she would.

"Just don't overlook the other verse, Nic," Doug said as he broke free from the forest and ran under God's unending light, pulling him closer, urging him faster, commanding he come. "And now these three remain: faith, hope and love. But the greatest of these is love."[2]

"Hold on to Rachelle's dream, Nic. Stand firm and be strong. Father will give you revelation. Love remains, Nic. Love remains!"

ᕼᓇ

When Rachelle called, I was at Gram's trying to sort through the aftermath when the phone rang. I'm sure my mind did what it always did when the phone rang – it played tricks on me.

"It's Doug. I have to get that," I said to myself.

They say if a survivor doesn't see the body of their loved one the brain cannot comprehend the loss for some time. I experienced that first hand. Whenever the phone rang my immediate thought was, "It's Doug." Once the memories flooded back my mind still refused to yield. "It's Doug," I would say to myself. "He's calling to tell me it was all a big misunderstanding."

So when the phone rang that day, I'm sure that's what I thought. Instead, it was Rachelle giving me the answer I had been praying for since May 25, 2006.

I wasn't asking "why" when the soldiers left my apartment, I was asking God about Heaven. The whys had come and gone with Simi's death. I wasn't questioning yesterday, nor did I ever get angry. My questions instantly focused on Heaven. Perhaps that's exactly what God wanted me to do. In fact, I know it was.

The vision of Heaven I had created wasn't the best. I think many of us are guilty of this false mentality. We think Heaven is going to be one big church service or at the very least singing praises all day long. Well, my husband was now in Heaven and I wanted reassurance I would be with him again.

I didn't know what to think of Rachelle's dream at first. When I put it on paper it seems silly that I ever doubted the answer to the question I had been repeating over and over in my head since the soldiers knocked on my door: "God, do I get remarried? I don't want to God; I want Doug. If I can have him there I will give up here. I will give up this life for the next. I will wait."

It took me months to come to the conclusion that I did, months on my knees before God with tears coursing down my cheeks. I questioned the dream and what it meant. I questioned if I understood it correctly or if I was taking something and twisting it into the response I desperately wanted to hear.

Although my answer was in those ten words uttered by Doug in Rachelle's dream, I continued to pray for insight, and God continued to answer, taking me step by step through my doubts and fears. Rachelle's dream was the first message after Doug's death I know came directly from God. I have had many since. God communicates differently for all people. I don't remember my dreams too often, but God uses Rachelle in this way. The secret for all of us, no matter how God speaks, is to pay attention. Humans have a way of discounting things, explaining them away as chance, coincidence, or just blind luck.

I don't believe in luck. I believe in God.

I don't know the whys and hows of eternity, but I do know this, thanks to Rachelle's dream: Doug is in Heaven and he loves me and wants to be with me just like he did on Earth. On the days I doubt I return to the dream. I replay Doug's words and hold on tight. But thankfully God isn't a God that talks once and leaves you alone to tread water. Every time you begin to sink, a buoy is thrown, a new, fresh, lifesaving buoy. Another one came just when the tides of doubt were closing in.

꩜

At Gram's house I kept my CD's in a cabinet in the living room, and Dak liked to open the cabinet drawers and pull out every single one. After saying "no" quite a few times to the little guy, Dak had grown accustomed to steering clear of the cabinet.

A few months after Rachelle had told me about her dream, I was sitting at the computer and Dak was once again invading the CD cabinet. I said "no" and went over to put a stop to things, thinking that was the end of the story. Later that day I was walking through the living room when a CD caught my eye. It was sitting on the coffee table, apparently one Dak had pulled out before I scolded him.

It made me stop in my tracks.

It was a homemade CD. Doug had written out all the songs in his not-so-fabulous handwriting. Of course, when you haven't seen your husband's handwriting in some time it stops your heart.

I picked up the CD as my eyes fell on the two songs in the second column — the only two songs in the second column.

Beautiful
Better Days

That alone caused my eyes to fill with tears. Doug called me Beautiful. That was how most of my letters were addressed and that was the first word he uttered when he came home — "Beautiful."

So I knew, without a doubt, Doug was either telling me to listen to the song "Beautiful," or he was saying, "Beautiful, listen to 'Better Days.'"

It was the latter.

The night before Doug's death we had talked on the phone, but it wasn't a great conversation. Doug was tired and I was distracted. It was well into the morning hours where he was and it was late night in Germany. Tara had something happen to her that day that upset her and I was between her house and mine, trying to help her sort it out. Before I went back to Tara's I made the decision to call Doug again (I had tried previously). I remember the delay was bad and I was frustrated that I couldn't talk to him easily. But I told him I loved him and he told me he loved me, as we always did, before we said goodbye.

I had been regretting that conversation. It had bothered me over the past months. Why didn't we talk longer? Why didn't I pour my heart out during that call?

I don't think there is any need to explain more. The song says it all. It's by the Josh Joplin Band.[3] The lyric's follow:

Better Days

Late night
Early morning
We talked until there was nothing left to say
It was strange
The war was on
But I've never felt so safe
And I've never seen better days

You laughed
You understood
Something unfamiliar
And I didn't think I could feel this way
I was cold and tired
And the world outside was hungry
But I've never seen better days better days
No I've never seen better days

And nights were tragic
But it didn't seem to matter
It was easier then to turn the other way
From the ruins of rage
I guess
We were scared
But I've never seen better days better days
No I've never seen better days

And when I kissed you
Concealing my confusion
Of what I knew but just couldn't say
I love you
I love you
Oh how I love you

And I've never seen better days better days
No I've never seen better days
The end is here
The end is here
The end is here
And I've never seen better days better days
No I've never seen better days

The song will break your heart. It did mine. It is intensely mournful yet strangely beautiful. I crumbled to my knees when I heard "I love you," and wept with despair when "the end is here" emanated from the stereo, but with that song came a realization I had never taken to heart. My Daddy knew what I needed and He would continue to reassure me if I would listen – and believe.

I don't recall ever hearing that CD or that song before that day, but there it was answering a question and calming my fears. Doug loved me and although the end was here he had never seen better days.

Your Daddy knows what you need and He never comes too late. No matter how long it takes you to receive the answer He has for you, He is right on time. When I found that song, I stopped questioning my last phone call to Doug. Doug knew exactly how I felt, and Daddy could use anything, including a song, to reassure me not only of Doug's love, but also of Daddy's faithfulness.

"Because of the Lord's great love we are not consumed, for his compassions never fail. They are new every morning; great is your faithfulness."[4]

And the messages continued to come.

༄

One morning I had just woken and was lying in the in-between mode of awareness and sleep. I wasn't thinking about anything, just existing.

Then a clear, strong voice in my head said, "Be faithful to me."

I froze, body and mind fully alert. The voice was as clear as a bell in the dead of winter. "Be faithful to me," it said.

Then that morning God gave me a scripture. If I had read it the day before it wouldn't have meant anything to me.

"Let love and faithfulness never leave you; bind them around your neck, write them on the tablet of your heart. Then you will win favor and a good name in the sight of God and man."[5]

The questions in my head were still not firmly answered. The question of "do I wait" was still not resolved. I continued to doubt what Daddy was telling me — and then this verse.

At that same time I was reading a book that said everyone has an assignment from God. I had journaled just days prior how I wanted to know what God wanted me to do. I firmly believe holding on to love and faithfulness is my assignment from God. "Let love and faithfulness never leave you." I don't know why, but remaining loyal to Doug will glorify God. Perhaps my insistence that "I'm waiting for Heaven" will give people something to think about.

Love never ends; that's what the Bible says. I thought Rachelle's dream would be the last message I would receive from Doug. When I played the "Better Days" song and heard "Be faithful to me" I realized I was wrong. I didn't think anything would be more of a blessing than that song or as perfect as that verse. I realized buoys would come but I didn't realize a lifeboat was on its way.

∽

Doug's best friend Jake and his wife Amanda came for a visit while I was still living at Doug's grandmother's house in New Hampshire.

Jake and Doug had attended West Point together and their bond was strong after graduation. I met Jake a few months after Doug and I started dating. Thankfully, Jake gave me his seal of approval, and lucky for me three years later Amanda entered Jake's life. A ball of energy that is all smiles and laughter, Amanda and I hit it off instantly. Although we had only seen each other twice before that fatal day, when Amanda received the news about Doug she crumbled to her knees. If anyone could feel my pain, it was Amanda. She was a constant presence in my life for years after Doug's death, sending me gifts and making surprise appearances that brought me a great deal of comfort.

When they arrived at Gram's, I asked Jake if he would help decipher Doug's palm pilot. It had come back from Iraq with everything erased. I was shocked but not surprised. The army does those things when critical information might be saved in the memory, but I was disappointed anyway. Doug stored music and pictures on his palm and I wanted to see what he was looking at during his final hours.

Jake linked the palm with my computer and asked me what I wanted to download. I knew I wanted Microsoft Outlook because Doug had entered all our friends addresses in it a year before he left.

When Jake unplugged the palm and handed it to me it was on the "notes" page instead of the "start" page as it was normally; there were two notes saved. One note was titled "I love you;" the other was titled "wonderful woman."

You can imagine my shock. I clicked on each one — they were blank, save for a small symbol at the top.

Jake was talking to me but I couldn't make out what he was saying. I couldn't focus on anything other than those two notes. I kept clicking on the screen, trying to discover, what, if anything, was saved there. From my perspective they were just two blank notes. I finally handed the palm back to Jake.

"What are these?"

Jake turned back to the computer and opened the notes page. He clicked on the first note and saw the symbol in the top left hand corner. Of course, he knew instantly what it was.

"It's a sound file."

I was confused. "What do you mean a sound file?"

He clicked on the sound icon. Doug's voice came out of the computer. "I love you."

Jake clicked on the second note.

Doug's voice said, "You're the most wonderful woman in the whole world, I love you very much."

I started sobbing. Amanda put her arm around me, "Nic, you didn't know?"

I shook my head as a question surfaced. "When did he record them?"

Jake looked up the properties to each document. "November 2, 2005."

He recorded them seventeen days before he left.

I almost couldn't believe it. Doug had recorded the messages but never told me about them. I would have played them every day of his deployment if I had known they existed. Why in the world would he have recorded them? In case he didn't make it back? But then, how did he know I would find them?

None of those questions really matter, but they go through your head.

When you get a gift like those messages you fear losing them. As soon as Jake and Amanda left I bought two frames that could record voice messages. The frames worked differently than any I had seen before. Instead of pushing a button at the bottom of the picture to hear the message, you actually pushed part of the picture itself.

When you record a message to these frames you hit the record button in back, speak your message, and then press an area on the picture to imprint that message. When you want to play your message you have to hit that particular spot on the picture. So, for instance, if you frame an image of a computer keyboard and you hit the letter D to record your message, when you want to reply that message you have to hit the letter D. You can't hit K, or E, or F or C or any other letter in the alphabet; you have to hit D.

After recording the messages on the frames, I put one in my living room and the other in my bedroom. I honestly didn't think it could get any better than those messages. What could God possibly allow that would be better than those words?

I had just bought a house in Doug's hometown. As I sat on the living room floor sorting through some of my things the frame talked by itself.

"You're the most wonderful woman in the whole world, I love you very much."

I stopped, looked up, and started crying. Then I wondered, "What just happened?" I walked over to the frame. Nothing was around it or touching it. Nothing was even near it. My windows were open but there was no breeze. My cat was beside me at the time. There was no reason for the frame to talk.

I sat down and thought, "Am I nuts? Did that really happen?"

Five minutes later it happened again.

I went over to the frame and sat by it until I went to bed. It didn't speak again, but at that point it didn't matter. Doug had just found a way to tell me he loved me with his own voice and my Daddy had let him.

∽

Now the frame talks all the time. Sometimes it doesn't talk for months, other times it talks ten times a night.

Some people say it must be the lights above it or movement around it that cause it to speak, but that isn't correct. At times the lights aren't on and it speaks. At times in the dead of night is speaks. It talks because my God allows it to. Most of the time it's the same message, "You're the most wonderful woman in the whole world, I love you very much." But sometimes it is the other message, the simple message of "I love you."

I hold fast to those "I love you" messages because I know that message is rare.

The first time I heard that particular message I was watching someone on television say they didn't think the men who died in Iraq were heroes. I was about to gouge the eyes out of this individual when the frame spoke the simple message of "I love you." It was as if Doug were saying, "Calm down, Nic. It just really doesn't matter does it? God will have the final word."

Then it happened again on Christmas night 2007. My company had just left and I was feeling horribly depressed when the frame spoke the simple message of, "I love you." With that message I knew everything was going to be all right: Doug was still there, God was still there, and although my life wasn't okay, my destiny was.

A verse now comes to mind.

"The Lord is close to the brokenhearted and saves those who are crushed in spirit."[6]

Yes, He is. He is close to me, allowing me to hear words that my husband wants me to know. He is a wonderful God to allow that. He knows what you need when you need it. What He does saves me, not only on this broken Earth, in my shattered spirit, but He saves me for His own, for eternity, and for my Doug.

My God is wonderful. I hope you know Him.

CHAPTER SIX

Our Journey

"For God so loved the world that he gave his one and only Son, that whoever believes in him shall not perish but have eternal life."

John 3:16

When Doug and I first met, he was studying a book about God that a classmate had given him. Although Doug believed God existed, he didn't feel the need to attend church. He had grown up Catholic, and to him the Catholic service left something to be desired. Instead of attending Sunday school as other denominations, you attended catechism, which is more doctrinal and not an in-depth study of scripture. Doug didn't like doctrine; he had enough formalities in the army. He didn't see God in the church; he saw God on the mountaintop. Why attend church when he could take a hike? The church itself did nothing for him.

I had a similar outlook, although vastly different circumstances. I had grown up a "mutt" of sorts. I had joined a Baptist church where my mother taught Sunday school but attended a Lutheran school until the eighth grade. By my freshman year in high school, the Baptist church had a disagreement among its members and split. Mom thought the rift childish and decided it was time to switch churches.

We started attending a Methodist service but I didn't know many people and failed to get involved in the extra curricular activities of the church, including Sunday school.

Looking back on my life, this lack of church involvement was a big mistake. In the Baptist church I was grounded in scripture. At one point my Sunday school teacher lectured us on reading the Bible. His speech had an immediate and lasting impact; I went home, turned to Genesis, and started reading. I was twelve. When I finished reading the Bible, I read it again. By the time I entered high school I had read the Bible cover to cover at least twice, did daily devotionals, and had a good grasp of my faith.

But as I slipped away from Sunday school and church activities I crept into a shallow faith. By the time I entered college and started dating someone who didn't have strong faith, it was easy to be led by the New Age movement which said, "You don't need church to believe in God."

Then I met Doug, and with both of our experiences we didn't feel pulled to attend church immediately. I told him we needed to find a church we both liked, and he agreed, but that never really blossomed into a full-grown desire until the morning of September 11, 2001 when I saw the second plane hit the Twin Towers. That morning was a very intense time for me, not only because I was an American, but also because I was the newlywed wife of a soldier. My husband might be going to war.

Doug's unit wasn't called after 9/11, but the desire to attend church became a must for me. I set out to find a contemporary service, but at the time they were hard to come by. I finally discovered a Lutheran church with a semi-contemporary worship style. Although Doug agreed to go with me, most Sundays he would look at me quizzically and ask, "Do we have to go?"

He loved me, so he went.

In my spare time at home I started reading my Bible again. I not only read it once, but twice, even three times. I ordered commentaries on scripture. I read anything I could find about Jesus. My prior fire came back, this time with much more force.

After three years in Fairbanks, Alaska we moved to Columbus, Georgia and rented a house with a church right across the street. The first day at that church we met friends we would have for a lifetime. We were only stationed in Georgia for nine months but that church helped save Doug.

I started teaching Sunday school, and my first lessons were on why the Bible was true. It was an interesting study that talked about the archeological and theoretical evidence of our faith. Most days, as we walked back home, Doug would continue asking me questions. By this time I knew enough to answer them.

Our friends had also just started a Bible study on the gospel of Luke; Doug wasn't only hearing evidence on why the Bible was true, he was also learning about the amazing person of Jesus.

During our time in Columbus I continued to study scripture, loving God with every piece of my being, but there was always a nagging question, "Was I okay with God? Was I God's child?"

As I have said, I grew up believing in God. I never questioned His existence or what Jesus had done for me, but I had my share of backsliding years. So, was I okay? I didn't know. The Baptist church we had attended when I was younger did great damage to my confidence because I heard multiple times, "If you don't know the day and the hour you were saved, then you aren't saved."

That terrified me. I had never walked to the front for the "altar call." There wasn't a time in my life I could point to as being the moment God graced me with salvation.

One day I got down on my knees after reading my Bible lesson. I remember saying through the tears, "God, am I okay with you? I need to know if I'm okay with you."

I don't know what I expected, but I didn't expect a voice in my head. My prayer had been heartfelt but it lasted mere seconds.

The voice was undeniable. "Isaiah," it said. I stopped praying, opened my Bible, and turned to Isaiah. Then I heard, "Forty-three."

This "command" had never happened to me before. I had never heard a verse in my mind and then flipped to the passage. It was a completely new experience.

I had just finished reading a book called *"The Name"* by Franklin Graham. One of his main points is how important a name truly is. Of course, he was talking about the name of Jesus but it made an impression on me. Graham stated if you hear Jesus' name you can't help but stop. Your heart can't help but jump. Test it, you will see. No other name does that. Only Jesus. Why? Because He is God.[1]

So I flipped my Bible open to Isaiah 43.

I looked at the first verses and immediately knew it was God's reply to my heartfelt question of, "Am I okay?"

God replied, *"Fear not, for I have redeemed you; I have summoned you by name; you are mine. When you pass through the waters, I will be with you; and when you pass through the rivers, they will not sweep over you. When you walk through the fire, you will not be burned; the flames will not set you ablaze. For I am the Lord, your God, the Holy One of Israel, your Savior."*[2]

He called me by name.

It was more than I could have hoped for. My God had taken a book I had just read and used it to assure me I that I was redeemed, I was summoned, and I was His.

Little did I know that the rest of the verse also pertained to what I would soon experience less than three years later. I would walk through the waters, the rivers, and the fire but I would not be swept over, and I would not be burned.

After finding a church we loved in Georgia, it was hard to transition to the formality of the service in Germany, but we faithfully went to a military chapel just down the road from our apartment. I was pregnant at the time, and when Dak was born there were days I just didn't want to get dressed for church. I would utter the same words Doug used to say in Alaska, "Do we really have to go?"

Doug would respond, "Yes, we do."

My faith hadn't failed, just my new-mother motivation. Rachelle and I had even started a Bible study that would grow to be almost ten people before I left, but with a one-month old sometimes it was a struggle to wake early and make the trek in the cold to the church. But Doug said we had to go.

Hallelujah!

One day we were walking back to our apartment when I asked a simple question that had been bothering me for quite some time. Although Doug always took the communion "body" of Christ, he never took the "blood." There was something fundamentally wrong with that in my mind. Why take one and not the other? Did he not fully believe? I needed Doug to believe. I needed him to take the blood.

"Why don't you take the blood in communion?" I asked.

"I don't know," Doug said, shrugging. "I just never have."

Then I had an epiphany. In Catholic services they drink out of the same cup. Perhaps Doug thought it was a little unsanitary. Most Protestant services serve every individual their own mini-cup, as did the church we currently attended. He had no excuses.

"Is it because you have to drink out of the same cup in the Catholic Church?" I asked, studying his profile as he pushed Dak in the stroller.

Doug glanced my way as he thought about the question. He nodded. "Yes, that's it."

"But Doug," I said, "they serve you in individual cups at this church. You have to take the blood of Christ. That's what covers your sins. You have to take the blood!"

The next time our church held communion, Doug took the blood. He didn't say anything about it, but I knew he had thought it through. Although the communion grape juice won't change your salvation it is an outward show of belief, a confirmation that you know the body of Christ was broken for you and His blood was shed for your sins.

"But he was pierced for our transgressions, he was crushed for our iniquities; the punishment that brought us peace was upon him, and by his wounds we are healed. We all, like sheep, have gone astray, each of us has turned to his own way; and the Lord has laid on him the iniquity of us all."[3]

Then we were transferred to Baumholder, Germany. Although the church wasn't the family as it had been in Georgia, it was far more personal than the one we had attended in Heidelberg.

Before Doug left for Iraq, the chaplain called all the soldiers who were deploying to the front of the church to pray over them. Many of the men went forward, but some remained in their seats. Doug didn't hesitate; he arose and went forward.

When I saw my husband huddled in that group of men I knew with every piece of my soul two years prior he wouldn't have risen from his seat. I can still picture him standing there in his orange shirt and dark khaki pants with his head bowed and hand on the man standing beside him.

I started sobbing. I tried to stop, but I couldn't help myself.

The girl beside me scooted over and put her arm around me.

"He's going to be okay," she said.

She thought I was crying because I was worried Doug wouldn't make it back from Iraq. But that wasn't it at all.

Of course he would be okay. No matter what happened, he would be okay.

I knew my husband believed.

❦

Doug laughed as he ran, the wind burning his face as his feet curled in the earth, digging into the velvet sand lining the river of life that ran from the throne of God and drifted into the lush green valley. Trees lined its banks, plush and full, ready to burst with fruit that would feed the nations.[4]

Saints surrounded him, all running with equal exhilaration, their collective shouts of enthusiasm mingling with the chorus of angels.

The angelic lights above him twirled toward the New Jerusalem, like thousands upon thousands of dandelion seeds set free in a torrential wind.

The clouds stared to billow in the distance, anticipating the things to come. Deer, lions, leopards, and all kinds of animals were intertwined among the saints, all moving forward with resolve, as if the gates of the New Jerusalem were a magnet, drawing them closer, wooing them to come witness the final confrontation between Satan and the Lamb.

Doug's toes curled, gripping the sand, pushing him further, closer to the brink of Heaven: the rim that started on the other side of the river of life, spreading out like a sea of glass, made specifically for this purpose – to let the saints be part of the rising escalation.

The coming years for those on the Earth would be frighteningly normal, yet increasingly horrific.

None of the wicked would understand, but the saints, those listening and following God, would recognize the signs and prepare.[5]

Doug jumped over a rock, landing like a cat on the other side, digging into the luxurious sand with his hands.

Life on Earth was a grain of sand. When you were in it, running though it, working and striving to achieve some measure of peace, life could seem like a frantic race with a definite end, but if you place that grain of sand on the ocean shore you realize how long you have yet to live.

Eternity.

The human mind couldn't grasp it. He couldn't grasp it as he walked through his own life. But God could. God could look at each individual life as a grain of sand tumbling and spilling over rocks, getting pounded in the reef, tossed by the waves. He could also see the beach and know, one day soon, that grain of sand would land and stop and rest. The waves would depart, the wind would cease, and the rocks would melt. God knew how to shape each grain of sand to become part of His shore.

"Hold on Nic," Doug said. "A couple more waves, a couple more storms, but the beach is ahead. The beach is ahead!"

༺༻

Doug's mother and stepfather took the immediate family on a trip the year following Doug's death. While I was packing for the trip to Florida, I realized I needed to find another book to take with me. I suddenly remembered the workbook Doug had been reading when we first met. It was called, *Experiencing God: Knowing and Doing the Will of God* by Henry T. Blackaby and Claude V. King.[6]

I have very vivid memories of seeing that workbook during our months of dating. I am fairly certain the day I first asked Doug about his belief in God he was reading that book, which is probably what prompted my question.

When I drew the book from the shelf, I flipped it open and immediately recognized Doug's handwriting. I read the question he had responded to:

In what are you investing your life, your time, and your resources? Make two lists below. On the left list things that will pass away. On the right list things that have eternal value.

On the left Doug wrote: clothes, house, furniture. On the right he wrote: love, God, good deeds, helping others.

For the eternal value question, the first thing he thought about was love. At times I wonder if he answered that question the day I asked him about God. We were soaking in the sun in my backyard. We were happy. We were in love.

Well, as soon as I saw Doug's words, I started crying; then my spirits lifted. Here was a book of 219 pages filled with questions. I could learn more about my husband, more about how he thought and felt about God, by studying the book.

I flipped through the other 218 pages. Doug didn't respond to any other question.

The eternal value question quoted above wasn't on page one; it was on page 48.

Coincidence? I don't believe in coincidence. I believe in love.

❧

Doug approached the western gate of the New Jerusalem, stunned by its brilliance. On Earth, he never liked fences or walls. They always seemed too confining, too territorial. But the translucent shimmer of the New Jerusalem's gates whispered a welcoming invitation and a promise of peace. A tall angel stood by the gate, serving as a reminder to the saints that no evil could touch them here.

The angel's face was strong, his jaw set, yet there was a slight smile to his face and a gleam in his eye that made Doug pause in admiration of his Father's creativity.

You could instantly distinguish a human from an angel, although angels had the same features and the same build. They were, well, more. They radiated the glory of God in such a way it was almost devastating. With sudden wonder, Doug realized it was because the angel standing before him had never sinned. There was no residue, not even a memory, of the fall. This creature had never had a negative thought, never acted out of rash impulsiveness, never thought to question the Father, reject the Son, or refuse the Spirit.

As the saints continued to hurry past, Doug perused their faces. These people had questioned the Father, at times rejected the Son, and even blatantly refused the Spirit yet they were allowed through the gates, into the walls, and past the watchful angel because of Jesus' sacrifice. Doug bowed to his knees, hands on the smooth, translucent pearl gate and thanked his Savior. When he paused to look back at the angel, the creature was studying him with intense interest. With slight amusement Doug realized the angels marveled at man just as much as man marveled at them. He had sinned, he was stained, and yet he had chosen truth and stood for righteousness.

Doug nodded; the angel nodded back, his slight grin deepening as he turned his attention back to the oncoming saints.

Doug ran his fingers over the walls, formed of crystal clear jasper so transparent you could peer through them as if you were looking through a pure mountain stream. On the other side of the wall, people purposely moved toward the far side of the city where the sea of glass extended from God's throne. There, the saints in Heaven would witness the final events on Earth.

Doug moved into the crowd of saints. The urgency he had first felt at the sound of the ram's horn was still there, pulling him steadily toward his Father's presence.

Everyone was moving quickly, laughing and talking to those beside them, everyone save one.

A man sat on an unadorned bench, back against the clear jasper walls. His robe was hiked up slightly, revealing the start of the man's slender legs. A thick silver band encircled his head, but it held no inscription, and his robe was belted simply with a leather cord. Although his appearance was modest something about the cut to the cloth and the craftsmanship of the accessories made Doug realize all items were costly.

Doug had never been a good judge of physical beauty, but if the man had lived in the days of Hollywood it would have been tragic not to see him on the big screen.

Wavy brown hair framed a slender yet masculine face. His strong jaw whispered resolve and his purposeful poise spoke volumes to the man's identity.

Every male in Hollywood would have paled in comparison. No wonder Nebuchadnezzar chose this man to be the leader of the wise men.

Daniel's gaze shifted to Doug.

Dark penetrating brown eyes studied him with deep insight. The wisdom in Daniel's look sent a shiver down Doug's spine. Despite his newfound knowledge here, the man sitting before him held an intelligence few others ever achieved. Daniel was the man who had dreamed the prophetic dreams Nic cherished. Daniel was a man "highly esteemed" by God.[7]

His look was consuming, yet welcoming. Although no smile graced Daniel's lips, Doug paused in his haste toward the sea of glass. Although his Father's pull was strong, and he could sense it just past the circle in which he now stood, somehow he knew Father wanted him to meet the man sitting before him.

Daniel watched Doug approach with silent introspection before he rose and bowed in greeting, as was customary in his day. Before Doug could do likewise Daniel shook his head and chuckled. "She won't stop asking God for wisdom, Doug. She doesn't realize once you start shaking that tree, more than one apple will fall."

Daniel's smooth voice was almost as commanding as his presence. With that voice mysteries were solved and questions were answered.

Doug was about to ask Daniel of whom he spoke when he realized the prophet referred to Nic.

"I asked for wisdom as well," Daniel continued. "If you seek it, Father will never disappoint. But at times Father's revelations are isolating. When she stands for her beliefs many will question the sanity of her convictions."

Doug knew Daniel spoke the truth. He could already feel Nic's unease when those surrounding her began to doubt her thinking. She would have to grow stronger if she wanted to hold fast to what the Spirit was telling her.

Daniel looked at Doug curiously. "Didn't know I would have to wait so long to meet you. Didn't know you would fade from the Earth during the rise of the Antichrist's empire."

Although Doug had never put it in those words, now that he was with Jesus, he knew he had died fighting the rise of the final manmade system that would give birth to the Antichrist. Fundamental Islam was infiltrating every country in the world and its goal was global domination.[8]

How could you fight an ideology that didn't value life but glorified death with suicide bombings and global jihad? How could you fight a religion that didn't care if a boy strapped a bomb around his waist and detonated it in a crowd of innocent people?

"Who is like the beast? Who can make war against him?"[9]

Doug studied Daniel curiously. "You have been waiting to meet me?"

Daniel looked up at the cloud of angels hurrying past. "I knew we would be friends but I didn't anticipate an end time connection," Daniel said, wrinkling his brow in slight wonder at Father's timing. "See, when you arrive here, Doug, you become aware of future friendships and long for those friends with just as much fervor as the ones you knew on Earth. But Father doesn't reveal all things." At the mention of the Father, Daniel's lips curved in a slight smile. His eyes closed for an instant, silently worshiping the one who had esteemed him.

With Daniel's words Doug felt a warmth enter him; it was a warmth of a Father who cared for His children in such a way to mold two people hundreds of years apart to become perfect companions in His future kingdom. It was a vast love, the love of his Father, and it was a love that was just beginning to unfold.

"I can't wait for Nic to meet you," Doug said with a smile. "Your conviction has touched her deeply. She wants a heart like yours, able and willing to sacrifice, able and willing to stand for what's right."

Daniel smiled, and when he did, the smile reached his eyes. "I'm looking forward to meeting her too. I've been waiting for quite some time. I continue to pray that the glorious Father may give her the Spirit of wisdom and revelation that she so desires in order to know our Savior better, know this place better, and hold fast to the revelations already bestowed."[10]

Another blast from the ram's horn sounded, startling Doug. Doug turned to see the streets empty except for one tall man jogging their way.

Samson grinned as he stopped beside them. "Have you told him?" he said, nodding to Daniel.

"No," Daniel said as he continued to peruse Doug's face. "I think Doug already knows why he had to meet me."

Doug was about to protest when a thought struck him. "The fog. Are you on the other side of me?

"Not quite," Daniel smiled. "I'm two down from you, on the other side of Nic."

Doug's already present grin widened. Of course, he knew Father would put Nic with him for eternity, but he hadn't yet formed the thought into a whole. He looked between Samson and Daniel. "So we will explore the stars together?"

"Perhaps you two could lead Nic and me on a journey of Father's creation," Daniel said, "and Nic and I could lead you two on a journey of Father's Word."

Samson released a huge belly laugh before growing serious. "It's sad. The enemy has taken eternity and twisted it to be something tedious. With the Carpenter every day is an adventure."

Daniel's smile faded. "Yes, Father made us. He knows what each of us desires. He is the one who has put those desires in us."

The call of the ram's horn caused all of them to look toward the far side of the city. Doug once again felt their Father's pull and their Savior's invitation as Samson turned to go. "Well, hurry now, we can't miss the beginning of the end."

Daniel followed the warrior and motioned for Doug to do the same. "The end won't start until all the saints are present. Father knew we had to meet Doug first."

The warmth entered Doug again, like the feeling of Christmas morning when the house was a mess of boxes and wrappings, yet smelled of freshly baked bread and was alive with children's laughter. It was the warmth of friendships long established which would continue to grow and develop into even more intimacy with each and every day. It was contentment, utter contentment, with where things were and where they would ultimately go. It was his Father's glory, his Savior's grace, and friendship, limitless friendship. Two bonds had already begun to grow, and they would only increase in intensity as eternity began.

As Doug followed Daniel, he realized he could hardly wait until Nic was perfected. He couldn't wait for her to meet the friends she would have for an eternity.

Father's pull suddenly became electrifying. Daniel quickened his steps and Doug did the same. Samson's laughter carried on the wind as they continued their haste down the street of gold, following the crowd of saints that had gone before them.

෨

There are things you remember more clearly when tragedy happens. A few incidents, in particular, stand out in my mind.

The first was when Doug and I were dating. We were driving back from a hike when Doug asked, "Do you think there's one person you're supposed to be with?"

I remember studying his profile, trying to decide what exactly he believed. I thought about it carefully before I replied, "I believe there are many people you are compatible with, but only one person you are supposed to be with."

He nodded and said, "I think so too."

When an answer like that comes from a man of character you know he has been evaluating the question for quite some time. I can just imagine Doug rising for an early morning run, miles away from me, and taking to the pavement, pondering our relationship and trying to decide whether or not we were made for each other.

The second was about a year before Doug deployed; I looked at him and asked, "Would you get remarried if I died?"

It is a pointless question really. If your spouse says yes, you would feel somewhat depressed; if they say no, you wouldn't believe them.

I can't tell you why I asked it that day, but I do know how Doug and I lived, or I should say how I decorate the house. I love pictures, not pictures of scenery, but pictures of the people I love. One of the first comments people make when they walk though my door is "Wow, you have some great pictures."

And I do.

I surrounded myself with pictures of Doug and Dak even before that fatal day. It is what I loved then and it is what I love now. Although my pictures have increased now that I can't see my husband anytime soon, it is a part of who I have always been.

So, if I had to guess, I was looking at our pictures and envisioning the worst-case scenario — what if one of us wasn't there?

So I asked the pointless question. Doug's answered immediately.

"No."

I stared at him for a minute, slightly shocked and somewhat speechless. I hadn't been expecting that response. I thought Doug would at least give the question some serious thought. I remember laughing and teasing him about it, insisting he didn't know what he was talking about. That surely he would remarry.

He didn't even try to argue with me, so I made a request. "If you do remarry, just keep a picture of me in the house."

Why would I say that? One picture? But as I said, pictures are important to me. I needed reassurance he would have a constant reminder of our life together.

It is interesting I remember that conversation. What I find more interesting is that Doug didn't even hesitate when he gave his answer. Would he get remarried?

"No."

It was firm. It was final. There was no room for discussion.

He would not get remarried.

Now that the worst has happened, I know how I would reply. As I have said previously, the question of remarriage was at the forefront of my mind as soon as those soldiers knocked on my door. It was the question I thought on most. It was the question I prayed on most. It was the question that led me to search the scriptures about Jesus' return, the Millennial Kingdom of Christ, and eternity. It was the catalyst that started my newfound zeal for the book of Revelation.

Some time after Doug's death I went to a wine tasting with some friends in Doug's hometown of Plymouth. A girl approached me and asked if I was Doug's wife. She had attended high school with him and had some good things to say about him during our brief conversation. One of her comments was, "It must be very hard to raise a one-year-old by yourself."

I replied, "It's better than getting remarried."

She was the first person to whom I spoke my thoughts out loud. I believe it was because she was someone I would probably never see again. I wouldn't have to argue my decision with a stranger.

I knew most of my family would say, "Oh Nic, don't say that. You're young and attractive; you'll find happiness with someone else." They would say that out of love of course, but to be honest, that's not what I needed to hear. I had to get rooted in my decision. I couldn't have any doubts enter my mind. Remarriage was something I had prayed about for almost a year, over and over, day by day, on my knees with tears coursing down my cheeks.

"God," I said. "Do I wait?"

The girl's reaction was how I imagine many people might respond.

"That's sad."

But it's not. Sometimes I sit and ask God "why me?" Why did you choose me to be so blessed?

My God still allows my husband to tell me "I love you" in his own voice. My God talks to me now more than ever. My God's messages continue to come. I don't want to miss one for all the gold in the world.

If I dated I wouldn't be who I am. I am Doug's wife; I am God's child who is now looking forward to Heaven; I will look up and wait because one day I will see Doug again.

When that day comes Doug will take my face in his hands and say, "You waited."

And I will say, "Yes, I did."

God is right there, whispering to our hearts, "Believe Me; trust Me; I can do anything."

One saying keeps going over and over in my mind. I believe it is from God: "Wait and see what I can do," He says. "Wait and see what I can do!"

Doug and Dak, hiking in Garmisch, Germany October 2005, one month before Doug deployed. This is the picture I was looking at when the soldiers notified me.

(L-R) Me, Doug, Amanda and Jake Miller, Doug's best friend and his wife, taken early 2004.

The Georgia Gang at our Columbus house before we left for Germany. April 2004. (Top L-R) Me, Amanda, Beth, Melvin, Brad, Doug, and Nathan. (Bottom L-R) Kevin, Jennifer and Rachel.

Heidelberg Friends at Christmas Dinner 2004. (L-R) Rachelle, Scott, Me and Doug.

Doug and Dak, a few months before Doug deployed. 2005

The girls of Baumholder, Germany in April 2006 on my birthday. (L-R top) Jan, me, and Jessica; Karen, Tara and me. (L-R bottom) Erin, me, and Kristine: Joanna, me, Paige and Erica.

Me and Doug – Dinner out in September 2005. (Photo taken by Jan, one of the Baumholder girls - the one with the obnoxious laugh like mine! Hee hee)

Me, Doug and Dak, the night before Doug left for Iraq. November 18, 2005.

Doug in Kuwait with Charlie Company, 2nd Battalion, 6th Infantry Regiment. 2006.

Doug having fun in Kuwait. 2006

(L-R) Specialist Robert Blair (Commander's gunner), Commander Doug DiCenzo, and Specialist Matthew Owens (Commander's driver). Robert Blair was KIA with Doug. Owens still suffers from injuries. Second Lieutenant Justin Watson (the Company's Fire Support Officer) isn't included in the picture but was also wounded in the blast. (Photo given by Wayne Hall)

Me and Dak at my mom's house Christmas 2005. Sending a picture message to Doug downrange – Hurry Up! (Photo taken by Nic's mom, Sherry Kitts)

The flag that greeted me at Doug's funeral in Plymouth, NH in June 2006. The Georgia Gang is walking toward me. (L-R) Rachel, Brad, Nathan and Amanda. (Photo taken by Nic's mom, Sherry Kitts).

(L-R) Grant, Dak, Jessica and me at Gram's house in Plymouth, NH. Dec 2006.

The town of Plymouth, NH dedicated a bridge to Doug in May 2008. Dak and I are sitting by the stone monument that honors him. Thank you Plymouth! (Photo by Amanda Miller)

Me and Dak as we are now. DOUG ROCKS. (Photo by Jessica Flynn of Capture Photography; she is one of the Baumholder girls. Love you Jess!)

CHAPTER SEVEN

Wait

"For love is as strong as death, its jealousy unyielding as the grave. It burns like a blazing fire, like a mighty flame. Many waters cannot quench love; rivers cannot wash it away."

Song of Songs 8:6b-7a

Doug fell to his knees by the sea of glass with both anticipation and apprehension. The crystal blue sea spread out from God's throne and reflected the colors of the New Jerusalem with such clarity that when you first approached it you felt as if another city lay just underneath its surface.

But as Doug leaned over the edge the city disappeared and the happenings of the Earth below came into sharp focus.

Most of the saints on Earth were unaware the elect in Heaven knew what was transpiring on the world below. Nic was always on his mind, in the forefront. Her emotions and hopes he carried with him like a blanket. Her struggles became victories, and her defeats transformed her into a purer bride.[1] His Father carefully wove the thread of each individual's life and joined it to the tapestry of the entire redeemed. No human mind could grasp it until they arrived here, on the edge of eternity. Doug could now see the intricate details of the Father's work that spanned centuries. It was all coming together for a final conflict, the last struggle between Satan and the Lamb. He would now witness it in Heaven as Nic experienced it on Earth.

Religion was becoming blurred and false christs were appearing, leading many astray. Tribal conflicts were increasing and wars were threatening the entire world. Islamic terrorists were killing many in the name of their religion, saying they were doing a service for their god. Famines were increasing and earthquakes were escalating. Many were turning away from the faith, lured by the lusts of the flesh and false religious systems. Love in the human heart was growing dim, people too busy with their lives to care more than a few days for the plight of others. Only those standing firm on the rock of Jesus' promises would come through the rising tide of evil unscathed.[2]

The mood of the Earth was ripe for the harvest.

Doug turned to look at God's city, a stark contrast to the world below. Although Doug couldn't yet see God's throne, he could hear the creatures surrounding the throne lift their voices to the sky: "Holy, Holy, Holy is the Lord God Almighty, who was, and is, and is to come!"[3]

In the distance flashes of lighting shivered across the heavens. The air rustled with the flight of angels gathering at the foot of God's throne. The creatures' voices, the rumblings, and the flashes of lightings screamed in urgency.

Doug turned toward the Earth, his earlier anticipation rushing back. The saints on Earth were praying, Nic was praying. Many were being persecuted for their faith. Many more soon would be. But many were ignoring the signs of the times, explaining them away as chance or circumstance.

"Now learn this lesson from the fig tree: As soon as its twigs get tender and its leaves come out, you know that summer is near. Even so, when you see all these things, you know that it is near, right at the door."[4]

The door was opening.

The rumblings were beginning to escalate. The Earth shuttered.

One by one, other saints had gathered beside Doug in a silence so great it was loud. With the elect now on their knees Doug had a clear view of God's throne, which stood in front of the eastern gate to the New Jerusalem. The One who sat on the throne had the appearance of crystal clear jasper and scarlet carnelian. Doug couldn't see His face, the radiance emanating from the throne only allowing an outline of the figure who sat thereon.[5] But Doug could feel the Father's eyes on him and hear His inner whisper as His spirit left the throne and billowed around the redeemed. Tears rose in Doug's eyes as the love of the Father poured into him, refreshing him like no liquid ever could.

An emerald rainbow arched over the Ancient of Days, crowning the Father with regality. Flashes of lightning and peels of thunder erupted from the throne, electrifying the air surrounding Him. The four six-winged creatures remained rooted around the Father as they continued their unending chant, "Holy, Holy, Holy is the Lord God Almighty, who was, and is, and is to come!"

Doug had never seen creatures so frightening, yet so utterly beautiful in all of his days. The six-winged seraphim were covered with eyes, in front and behind, even upon their wings, reminding those present of God's all-seeing nature and eternal presence. The guilty would be punished and the righteous would be rewarded, but no deed, action, or thought had escaped the Ancient of Days. Each seraph had a different face, also representing God's dominion over every creature on the Earth. The first had the face of a man, the second an ox, the third a lion and the fourth an eagle. Their expressions were pure worship and their voices shear beauty.[6]

As the seraphim continued their song thousands of angels descended, causing the throne room to radiate a spectrum of light. As if of one mind the angels bowed to their knees, lips pursed in resolve, leaning forward in expectation, voices now hushed. Their silence so soundless it hummed.

Doug could feel Nic's faith increasing with each breath and with each message sent, and there were more coming, more than she could ever imagine. It was amazing how much more their love was growing now that they were apart. It was as if they were dating again, waiting in eager anticipation for their reunion on the weekends.

This reunion would have to wait a little longer, but it was coming. Nic could feel it. He could feel it. She just had to wait. He just had to wait.

Wait.

That was one of the messages God had sent from him. It was in a song in the child's Christmas cartoon *Cricket on the Hearth*.[7] But it spoke his heart.

> *Don't give your love away.*
> *Wait for me, I will come back to you.*
> *And we will have a thousand days of May*
> *Don't give your love away.*

Doug's eyes lifted to the sky as more angels drifted past. The sky was turning a deepening gray, and although God's light never left this place, the transformation was a stark reminder of the judgments to come. God's power wasn't something to ignore as many did. It was something to revere. The white of the angels stood in sharp contrast to the pulsating gray sky.

The creatures' voices were growing stronger.

"Wait, Nic," Doug whispered. "Almost time."

❦

As I have said previously, I wanted to be alone after everything happened. I knew I needed to pray and listen to Daddy.

"And if you call out for insight and cry aloud for understanding, and if you look for it as for silver and search for it as for hidden treasure, then you will understand the fear of the Lord and find the knowledge of God."[8]

After my screams diminished, I became still. In the stillness I read my Bible, and I prayed.

God tells us to pray without ceasing and I believe my continuous prayers helped guard my heart and mind from enemy attack. The enemy couldn't get a word in edgewise. If I wasn't internally screaming, "Daddy, help me," I was praying it, or I would say "Jesus, hold my hand," and then I would repeat Bible verses that comforted me time and again.[9]

"The Lord has made a proclamation to the ends of the earth: "Say to the Daughter of Zion, 'See, your Savior comes! See, his reward is with him, and his recompense accompanies him.'"[10]

"Be still before the Lord and wait patiently for him; do not fret when men succeed in their ways, when they carry out their wicked schemes."[11]

I prayed earnestly every day, "Tell me what to do God. If I can have Doug there, I will give up here. But don't tell me what I want to hear. I want the truth." Something in my soul screamed that I had to make the decision quickly or I wouldn't have the insight to do so in the future.

Although I desperately wanted God to tell me I would be with Doug again, no matter what I had to endure here, I feared His answer. I knew scholars insisted there was no marriage in Heaven. I knew many believed life in Heaven was nothing like life on Earth.

I didn't want to trust the scholars. I wanted to hear it from Daddy. If I needed to start my life again, I needed Him to give me a firm command. Based on what I had read, that was exactly what He would do. I thought He would tell me to move on and grow up. I thought He would tell me I needed to find happiness here with someone else.

I was in the moment, focused on God's response, tuned in to anything He said to me. The world and its desires were the farthest thing from my mind. I knew as time passed the more other influences would seep in, some even well-intentioned, pulling me to conform to their standards. I had to make a decision with Daddy's guidance. I had to have clarity of purpose. I had to have revelation.

I knew from scripture God would answer my prayer.

"God will always give what is right to his people who cry to him night and day, and he will not be slow to answer them."[12]

When I began to receive the answer I wanted, I worried I was jumping to conclusions. Was I hearing only what I wanted to believe?

During this season of questioning I met Brenda. Brenda had seen Doug's picture in the paper when I arrived in New Hampshire. She sat at her kitchen counter the day she read the article and sobbed. She didn't know me at the time, but she found a way to contact me after I arrived in Plymouth. She is one of my greatest gifts from God. Brenda gave Dak the Christmas Classics DVD set that contained the now cherished *Cricket on the Hearth* movie. It was a "freebie" in the set and wasn't originally supposed to come with the package. I found it odd there was an entirely separate DVD included which is what prompted me to sit down and watch it with Dak.

In the movie, a soldier leaves for war and tells his fiancée, "Wait for me; I will come back to you, and we will have a thousand days of May." That meant a lot to me because of the thousand-year reign of Christ. After Christ returns, the Bible says He will reign for a thousand years on Earth.[13]

A month after Doug's death I had journaled that I wanted to know more about the millennial reign of Christ. Throughout my Christian walk I had always been confused by the concept. A millennial reign? Why would Jesus want to "reign" for a thousand years before eternity began? Why would God find it necessary to carve out that period of time?

To further muddy the waters, Satan, who is bound at the beginning of the thousand-year reign, is re-released at the end of those years in order to deceive the nations once again.

Re-released? Deceive the nations? I thought we had "been there done that" so to speak. Why was God allowing the release of Satan when His Son had already been crowned King?

To make matters even more confusing, God the Father doesn't come to Earth with the New Jerusalem until after the millennial reign of Jesus. Only then does the old order of things pass away.[14]

Fascinating. But why?

Then came May 25, 2006 and my questions about Heaven. I had always assumed the thousand-year reign was something for God, to fulfill all prophecy and usher in peace on Earth, yet as I continued to pray God's answers contradicted what I had always been taught. To tell you the truth, before my husband met Jesus I wasn't excited about Heaven. Why would I be? I love Earth. I enjoy food and wine and fellowship. I adore animals and waterfalls and mountains. I didn't want to let Earth go. It was my home. I had even asked a chaplain about Heaven. He basically told me the life I had with my husband was, in fact, over.

Yet, the "wait" messages continued to come.

At church I heard messages on "waiting." In movies I happened to watch there was a theme of "waiting." Everywhere I turned, I felt like God was telling me to wait. The most substantial message came in Rachelle's dream where Doug indicated he wanted to be with me. Could that be in the way we were together on Earth? His words seemed to indicate just that.

Then Daddy gave me the "wait" message in *Cricket on the Hearth*, which specifically mentioned the word "thousand." I felt like God was pointing to the thousand-year reign of Christ. He seemed to be saying, "Nic, look at the Millennial Kingdom of my Son."

Was my former assessment about Heaven and the millennial reign wrong? Were the scholars wrong?

Then God gave me this verse: *"And after you suffer for a short time, God, who gives all grace, will make everything right. He will make you strong and support you and keep you from falling. He called you to share in his glory in Christ, a glory that will continue forever."*[15]

Scripture says God will make everything right. So I got to thinking; what if the millennial reign of Jesus was to right all the wrongs that had happened to God's people? Were those years a gift to us? I wondered and then I researched. I read everything I could find on Heaven. I searched the scriptures and started to study differing opinions on how the last days would play out.

My mind kept turning back to one fact. God had made everything right in the beginning. The Garden of Eden was paradise. Adam and Eve walked with God and had fellowship with Him.[16] There was no death, no tears, no crying, and no pain in Eden. God didn't create Adam and Eve to decay; He created them to live forever.

God gave them a directive before the end of the sixth day, while everything was still "good." This means God's command came before the fall, before sin, and before the curse of death.

What was God's directive? *"Be fruitful and increase in number; fill the earth and subdue it."*[17]

Adam and Eve were supposed to fill the Earth with children while their bodies were "perfect," without sin or death. Eve was meant to give birth and Adam was equipped to help her out a bit.

Adam and Eve had everything, a paradise on Earth, a new world to explore, and a Father who loved them and told them to fill the Earth with children. But our all-knowing God, in His ultimate wisdom knew Eden wasn't enough. Love isn't love without a choice. It is slavery. So He gave us the tree of the knowledge of good and evil.[18]

If you study the first three chapters of Genesis, you will come to realize God never told Adam and Eve about the tree of life, only the tree of knowledge. Why? Because they already had life! They had unbroken fellowship with their Creator. If they chose to remain near God they would frequent Eden and eat from the tree of life. If they wanted to be their own god and rebel against the perfect love that created them, they would choose to take from the tree of knowledge.

We all know how this story ends. Eve ate the tainted fruit and her husband after her. Death entered the world. But even then God stepped in and declared it wasn't the end. He would send a Savior. Now the choice of love was made manifest. Jesus came to Earth.

God loved us enough to give us a choice, knowing full well the choice would lead to sin, sin would lead to death, death would lead to a Savior, and the Savior would lead to salvation. Now there was a love that could never be broken – the love of a Savior laying down His life for the sinner. In turn those who choose to accept Jesus' sacrifice couldn't possibly fall out of love with their Redeemer. Not when He has given so much of Himself.

We made the choice to eat the fruit, but God gave us another choice – His Son. If we choose Him, and love Him, He promises death isn't the end.

"But your dead will live; their bodies will rise. You who dwell in the dust, wake up and shout for joy. Your dew is like the dew of the morning; the earth will give birth to her dead."[19]

That's what believers call the rapture.

The curse is broken. Now our choice leads to salvation because of a Savior who provides life for eternity and unbroken fellowship with God.

Eden comes again.

We call this Eden, Heaven.

But many Christians aren't looking forward to Heaven. We like Earth, and we like the order God has given us. To many, Heaven is something mysteriously unappealing. Why is it that most Christians when confronted with, "Are you excited about Christ's return?" stutter over their words, backpedaling faster than a five-year-old caught with his hand in the cookie-jar? "I'm not ready," most say, "I want to live my life. I want to see my kids grow up and get married. I want grandchildren. I want to die only when I have lived out my years. I want Jesus to wait."

It must break God's heart.

Heaven is what we are supposed to long for. "Thy Kingdom Come" is what we are supposed to pray for. Jesus' return is what we are supposed to look for. Heaven is not what we think it is. Heaven is everything we want. Let me say that again: Heaven is everything we want.

Why aren't preachers preaching Heaven? Why aren't we excited about it?

I will tell you why. There's an enemy who doesn't want us to look to Heaven and he has done a smashing good job of blaspheming God's dwelling place.[20] He has convinced most of us Heaven is boring. He wants us to live for a fallen world, his world, and not the future kingdom God has prepared for us.

What most Christians fail to realize, and what most preachers have failed to preach is just what Heaven is to us humans.

"I saw the Holy City, the new Jerusalem, coming down out of heaven from God, prepared as a bride beautifully dressed for her husband. And I heard a loud voice from the throne saying, 'Now the dwelling of God is with men, and he will live with them. They will be his people, and God himself will be with them and be their God."[21]

"Heaven comes to Earth," God whispers to our souls. "Heaven comes to Earth!"

∾

If Daddy says Heaven comes to Earth, wouldn't most Christians pause before they gave the stuttering reply of, "I'm not ready yet?" They would hesitate and wonder if Heaven comes to Earth, will Heaven be like the Earth I love?

Heaven is not some far off mystical world. Yes, at the rapture we will be in "Heaven" but we won't remain there. In Revelation 19 the saints are seen returning to Earth with Christ in the lead. We descend to cleanse the Earth of evil and set up Christ's Millennial Kingdom. Scripture even describes the world we return to claim: "The land is like the garden of Eden before them."[22]

It is like the Garden of Eden.

What does the believer's Heaven look like?

It is a renewed Earth.

It is Earth with a perfect King.

It is Eden reborn.

You might want to say, it is a glorified "do over."

Glory![23]

Isn't that just like God? "Lets see now children, lets see what we can do with my Son ruling from the throne. Those of you who have chosen Him wouldn't think of betraying Him would you? You have seen His love, My love, and you will never desire another god. I give you life, as it was meant to be, in the beginning!"

We live again. We live on Earth. We live with Jesus ruling the nations.

What Jesus doesn't want in His kingdom is sin. In the renewed Earth, we will live under Jesus' law — the perfect law. So let me ask you a question. Is the spousal relationship sinful? Is having children sinful? Is eating or drinking sinful? What about climbing a mountain or diving into a clear mountain lake? What about friendship and fellowship? None of the above is a sin. None of them.

But we have this vision of Heaven that has none of those things in it.

Why?

Think about it. Why?

Let's see what scripture says about the Millennial Kingdom. One of the best scriptures to look at is Isaiah 65:21-25.

"They will build houses and dwell in them;
they will plant vineyards and eat their fruit.
No longer will they build houses and others live in them,
or plant and others eat.
For as the days of a tree
so will be the days of my people;
my chosen ones will long enjoy the works of their hands.
They will not toil in vain
or bear children doomed to misfortune;
for they will be a people blessed by the Lord,
they and their descendants with them.
Before they call I will answer;
while they are still speaking I will hear.
The wolf and the lamb will feed together,
and the lion will eat straw like the ox,
but dust will be the serpent's food.
They will neither harm nor destroy
on all my holy mountain," says the Lord.

Did you know you would be building houses in the Millennial Kingdom of Christ? Yes, you will! You will build your house and it will be the house you always wanted.

Did you know you would be eating in the Millennial Kingdom of Christ? Yes, you will eat. In fact, you will feast! Everything you plant will blossom because scripture says you won't toil in vain.

Did you know there would be animals there? Each and every animal will be present and they will be peaceful. You will be able to ride on the back of a lion; you will be able to play with the bear; you will be able to swim among a school of sharks. And let me tell you about dinosaurs. Want to see them? You will! The Earth will be renewed and regenerated. Want to run with a T-Rex? Just wait. You will get your chance.

"Really, Nic," you say, "dinosaurs?" I want you to check out Job 41:14-26. It is talking about a creature called a "leviathan." Tell me, what kind of a creature does this sound like?

> Who dares open the doors of his mouth, ringed about with his fearsome teeth? His back has rows of shields tightly sealed together; each is so close to the next that no air can pass between. They are joined fast to one another; they cling together and cannot be parted. His snorting throws out flashes of light; his eyes are like the rays of dawn. Firebrands stream from his mouth; sparks of fire shoot out. Smoke pours from his nostrils as from a boiling pot over a fire of reeds. His breath sets coals ablaze, and flames dart from his mouth. Strength resides in his neck; dismay goes before him. The folds of his flesh are tightly joined; they are firm and immovable. His chest is hard as rock, hard as a lower millstone. When he rises up, the mighty are terrified; they retreat before his thrashing. The sword that reaches him has no effect, nor does the spear or the dart of the javelin.

Now if this isn't a fire-breathing dragon I don't know what is! This is a creature God was pointing out to Job, a creature Job could see! We will see that creature again. We will see it in the Millennial Kingdom of Christ. How do I know this? Because God said the world would be renewed. It will again be like it was in Eden.[24] Glory!

Did you know you would be bearing children in the Millennial Kingdom of Christ?

Many scholars will insist only the tribulation saints, those who are still alive at Christ's return, will have the privilege of repopulating the Earth.

Their logic goes something like this, "Because those who have died in Christ will receive perfected bodies at the rapture they won't be capable of bearing children."

Scripture is unclear when these tribulation saints will receive their perfected bodies, but for this argument it doesn't really matter. All we need to do is go back to Adam and Eve. They had bodies that were fashioned by the Almighty God to live forever and Daddy told them to fill the Earth with children. Their bodies were made to give birth.

Let me say that another way: perfected bodies were meant to give birth.

Satan is no fool. He takes God's beauty and perverts it to something grotesque. In today's world, sex is tossed around like candy at Halloween. It sells clothes, it sells movies, and it sells magazines, yet once you are married, it is spoken of in hushed whispers. I mean, isn't sex bad? That's what we have come to believe. So, when we think of glorified bodies, those that will live forever, we do not associate them with a spousal relationship.

Satan didn't create sex, God did. It was to be between one man and one woman. It was meant to draw them closer in the bond they would share as one flesh.[25] Marriage was also meant to produce godly offspring.[26] God intended for the marriage bed to provide a loving Creator with untold billions of children to spoil.

Other scholars argue marriage is only a representation of Christ and the church, hence when we are with Jesus we will no longer need the spousal relationship.

Lets turn back to Genesis chapter two, verse twenty: *"For Adam, no suitable helper was found."*

God was right there with Adam. Adam walked with God. Wouldn't that fellowship fulfill everything Adam needed? Well, God didn't think so. So what does God do? He fashioned Eve to fit Adam, and fit him Eve did. Woman was made for man before the fall. In every aspect of life, Adam needed Eve. God knew that, and God blessed that relationship.

But surely, you say, Adam never touched Eve until after the fall. Surely, in a perfect world that just couldn't happen.

Well, lets think about this for a minute. I wonder what Adam and Eve did on the seventh day? After all, it was supposed to be a day of rest. Adam looks at Eve, the first woman, stark naked, with a playfully silly grin on her face. I'm sure Adam kept his hands to himself. Have you ever wondered why Adam agreed to take a bite of that fruit? My friends, he wasn't about to let her go!

I am being a little silly with my illustrations, but I don't believe I have made any unsound observations. One man and one woman are God's plan, His original design and His original order. We are the ones who have distorted something beautiful and perverted it to something it was never intended to become. The marriage union was supposed to be an illustration of how Christ loves the church.[27] It was to be unbroken, cherished, and even longed for. Man is incomplete without woman. How do I know? God said so.

In the beginning, there was God. Six days later, there was Adam, but Adam was incomplete, so God made Eve. Then what did God say? *"For this reason a man will leave his father and mother and be united to his wife, and they will become one flesh."*[28]

God's order had begun.

In the beginning, at the fall, there was a lie. Satan has continued to lie to us. We don't look forward to Heaven because we don't look forward to losing the order we have on Earth.

We fear we will live without marriage. We fear we will have no more children. And what about the children we have now? Some believers think their children will be taken from them or even resurrected fully grown. We will never see our children married, never bounce grandchildren on our knee. We fear we will never eat again, drink again, or have a party. We fear we will never write that book we meant to write, or climb Mount Everest. We will miss out, won't we, in Heaven?

Why would we think that? God made this world. He declared it "good." There is no reason to think the "good" Daddy made is going to be ripped from our grasp. In fact, scripture says just the opposite. Daddy had a perfect plan in the beginning. We chose to deviate from that plan but Daddy is getting us right back on track. It is called the millennial reign of Christ.

In the Millennial Kingdom, children will be able to play with vipers and lead lions, inhabitants will be able to bear children without the fear of misfortune, the population will build houses and inhabit them, and they will never toil again in vain.[29]

Let's go back to Genesis chapter one. What does God say to Adam and Eve? What does He tell them to do?

"Be fruitful and increase in number; fill the earth and subdue it. Rule over the fish of the sea and the birds of the air and over every living creature that moves on the ground."[30]

Fill the Earth! Rule the Earth! Love each other!

In Revelation, the old order doesn't pass away until after the millennial reign of our Savior.[31] We have a millennium with the order we know and love.

Our life as we know it isn't over when we die. There is another phase to the believer's life. If you are crippled, you will dance. . . and live your life. If you are blind, you will see. . . and live your life. If you are insecure, you will be restored. . . and live your life. If you have miscarried a child, you will get to raise that child. . . and see that child live their life. This world cannot harm us. Why? We have the gift of the millennial reign of Christ.

Jesus tells us to store up treasures in Heaven. This life is a choice to walk with God. Adam and Eve could have walked away from "the tree of knowledge of good and evil." If they had done so they would have yielded their life to God. They would have indirectly chosen the tree of life, unbroken fellowship with God, and eternity. Yet, they wanted to be their own god, walk their own way, and live independently of Him. They chose to break the relationship.

We have that choice again. If we choose Jesus, we choose the tree of life, unbroken fellowship with God, a yielding of choice to God, and a complete surrender to the One who created the universe. If we do this we "lose" our life because we yield it to God. Yet, we also save it for eternity. What did Jesus say? *"For whoever wants to save his life will lose it, but whoever loses his life for me will save it."*[32]

If you're like me, the above scenario sounds very good. It sounds like just what you've always wanted. Yet, there is one scripture that keeps coming to your mind, isn't there? It's the one verse I kept dwelling on when Daddy continually told me to wait. "Daddy," I would say, "How can I wait when Jesus said: 'At the resurrection people will neither marry nor be given in marriage; they will be like the angels in heaven?'"

I would wager most of our fear of Heaven stems from this one verse. We like the order we have here, and this verse seems to indicate Heaven will be nothing like the Earth we know and love.

Let's look at that passage a little more carefully.

That same day the Sadducees, who say there is no resurrection, came to him with a question. "Teacher," they said, "Moses told us that if a man dies without having children, his brother must marry the widow and have children for him. Now there were seven brothers among us. The first one married and died, and since he had no children, he left his wife to his brother. The same thing happened to the second and third brother, right on down to the seventh. Finally, the woman died. Now then, at the resurrection, whose wife will she be of the seven, since all of them were married to her."[33]

Something about this sounds suspect, don't you think? First we are immediately informed the Sadducees didn't believe in the resurrection of the dead. They are asking about something they believed would never take place!

Let's make a modern day comparison. Jesus knows the Earth is round but is speaking to people who believe the Earth is flat. The flat Earth believers may ask Jesus something like: "Teacher, how many times could we circle the world until we fell off? One, two, or seven?"

Well, the premise of the question is false. If we believed the Earth was flat we couldn't circle the world at all. It is a question that intends to mock the responder. The Sadducees wanted to make a little fun of Jesus.

Now lets see Jesus' reply.

You are in error because you do not know the Scriptures or the power of God. At the resurrection people will neither marry nor be given in marriage; they will be like the angels in heaven. But about the resurrection of the dead — have you not read what God said to you, "I am the God of Abraham, the God of Isaac, and the God of Jacob"? He is not the God of the dead but of the living.[34]

Jesus cuts to the chase fairly quickly with, "You are in error because you do not know the Scriptures or the power of God." What is He saying here? "Sadducees," Jesus says, "you don't know my Father's word or His power. My Father's word says there will be a resurrection and my Father has the power to raise the dead. You are in serious error."

Then He touches briefly on the question asked, even though it is quite clear the question asked isn't the true question at all. Jesus says, "At the resurrection people will neither marry nor be given in marriage; they will be like the angels in heaven."

Scripture needs to interpret scripture. There is no other passage in the Bible that states we will be anything like angels. In fact, we will judge angels.[35] There is only one time we will be "like" the angels in Heaven, and that is when we are in the heavenlies at the resurrection of the dead. This ushering to Heaven is described by the apostle Paul: *"For the Lord himself will come down from heaven, with a loud command, with the voice of the archangel and with the trumpet call of God, and the dead in Christ will rise first. After that, we who are still alive and are left will be caught up together with them in the clouds to meet the Lord in the air."[36]*

Jesus even said, *"In my Father's house are many rooms; if it were not so, I would have told you. I am going there to prepare a place for you. And if I go and prepare a place for you, I will come back and take you to be with me that you also may be where I am."[37]*

So, at some point we are resurrected and are taken to God's throne. An in-depth study of scripture reveals that this transformation occurs before God's wrath falls on the unrepentant. While the wrath of God falls on Earth, we are in Heaven with Jesus but we don't remain there. God didn't make us for Heaven; He made us for Earth.

"I saw heaven standing open and there before me was a white horse, whose rider is called Faithful and True. With justice he judges and makes war. . . The armies of heaven were following him, riding on white horses and dressed in fine linen, white and clean."[38]

We return with Jesus at the end of time to cleanse the Earth of evil and be part of Jesus' millennial reign. Scripture says the Earth will be destroyed by fire, but this is not a total destruction, it is a surface cleansing.[39] Fire is destructive, but fire can also purify and refine.

"But who can endure the day of his coming? Who can stand when he appears? For he will be like a refiner's fire or a launderer's soap. He will sit as a refiner and purifier of silver."[40]

A refiner's fire removes the impurities and beautifies the object being refined. We will be made new, the Earth will be regenerated to Eden, and a perfect King will reign for a millennium.[41]

Back to Jesus' answer. At the resurrection, we will be in Heaven, and we will have yet to return to Earth and the order of Earth. We will be like the angels, awaiting God's fulfillment of end time events. We will be looking forward to the believer's Heaven – Earth reborn.

So at the rapture, at the resurrection, we won't be married or given in marriage. Why? We will be in the heavenlies awaiting Earth.

After Jesus gives His one-sentence response to the Sadducees lengthy misapplied inquiry about marriage, He continues to emphasize the Sadducees underlying question. "But about the resurrection of the dead – have you not read what God said to you, 'I am the God of Abraham, the God of Isaac, and the God of Jacob'? He is not the God of the dead but of the living."

Jesus knew their heart, and their mockery of the resurrection of the dead. He concludes by stating God is a God of the living, not the dead. Again, Jesus underscores, "You are in error. You do not know the power of God."

To my knowledge, this is the only passage biblical scholars use to say there will be no marriage in Heaven. It was based on a mocking question and it was answered specifically for the manner in which it was asked. The Sadducees only inquired about the resurrection, not the Millennial Kingdom, and certainly not eternity.

We all know the Millennial Kingdom and eternity will draw us closer to God. Let me ask you a question. When do you feel close to God now? Do your children make you love God more, or less? What about your spouse? What about sitting in front of a calm mountain lake and watching eagles soar over your head. Do these things draw us closer, or take us further away?

Of course they draw us closer. Worshiping God isn't always sitting in a church service: it is dancing, it is exploring, and it is loving.[42]

Worshiping God is living.

Let me say that again.

It is living.

Babies are being born during the millennial reign of Christ. I believe the meaning is twofold. I believe babies will still be conceived in the Millennial Kingdom of Christ by not only the tribulation saints, but for everyone God so chooses to reward in that way. Secondly, God has not forgotten those babies who have been aborted and miscarried, or children who have died young. They will have a chance at life in the Millennial Kingdom. They will have a choice to choose the perfect King who rules them. They too will grow in the Millennial Kingdom, and they will be able to live the life that was denied them. How do I know this? Because God said He would make everything right.

We have just discovered why Satan is re-released. Although children in the Millennial Kingdom grow up in peace, they have never had a chance to prove their love for God. Let me say that another way: there will be a population on the renewed Earth that has not had "the tree of knowledge of good and evil" experience. Satan will challenge them to make that final choice.

Those babies will grow under the perfect kingship of the Lord. They will witness first hand, just like Adam and Eve, His justice and love. During the Millennium, they will have a choice. Some will even die when they make the wrong choice. Lets look at Isaiah 65 verse 20.

Never again will there be in it an infant who lives but a few days, or an old man who does not live out his years; he who dies at a hundred will be thought a mere youth; he who fails to reach a hundred will be considered accursed.

This is how we know Isaiah 65 is talking about the Millennial Kingdom of Christ and not eternity – there is death there. Surprising? Yes, it is. I didn't think death was present after Jesus' return, but scripture says it is. Death is only abolished after the Millennium, when Daddy descends to the Earth with the New Jerusalem.[43]

What about those of us who are raptured or have tasted death before the Millennium? We have already chosen the Way, the Truth, and the Life. We have been tried and tested. We have eternal life in the Lamb. However, Isaiah 65 says those believers will be bearing children. Those born will still have to make a choice. Some will make the wrong choice. They will reject the rule of Christ and they will die. Scripture says those who do die will be thought "accursed." This means, they are cursed. What is the curse? Death! *"For the wages of sin is death, but the gift of God is eternal life in Christ Jesus our Lord."*[44]

There will be some who die during the thousand-year reign. Then, at the end of the Millennium, Jesus will give those remaining Millennium children a final choice, just like in the beginning of Genesis. Once again, Daddy knows love is no love at all without a choice. Satan will provide that final temptation.

Unfortunately, the Word says many will turn away from the absolute and total perfection of Jesus Christ on Earth. They will choose Satan. At the end of the millennial reign Satan amasses a large army "like the sand on the seashore."[45]

Christ doesn't allow this rebellion to last long. Even though Satan deceives the nations and His army surrounds the camp of God, there is no battle. God rains down fire and Satan's army is literally toast.[46]

It is finished before it ever began.

Then and only then does eternity begin. In eternity, scripture says the old order will pass away.[47] What this looks like we don't know, but in my mind, the new order cannot include childbirth. Why? If we were still bearing children in eternity, God would have to give those children a choice, and if humans have a choice they will fall. So, the order of Earth will not exist in eternity. Does this mean everything we know goes away? I don't think so. Everything God made is "good." This is when, I believe, the entire universe will be open to explore. I can't imagine wanting to explore the universe without Doug. He's my best friend. Daddy declared we are one flesh. I believe this is for eternity. I always have. That is why I engraved on Doug's wedding ring "ILU Always & Forever." I meant forever, not "until death do us part."

Once my questions about the Millennium were answered, Heaven came into focus and everything else started to fall into place.

My God telling me to "wait" made sense. The verses He had given me slowly started to form a whole.

God created a perfect world in the beginning. He has never lost sight of that goal. He has never given up the command, *"Be fruitful and increase in number; fill the earth and subdue it.*[48]

Daddy doesn't give up on a good plan. Daddy just says, "Wait."

He can make everything right. He can, and He will. What has happened in your life? What will Daddy make right for you?

It is just like God to give us a surprise like that. "A thousand years," He whispers. "A thousand years!"

CHAPTER EIGHT
The Train

"Behold, I am coming soon! My reward is with me, and I will give to everyone according to what he has done."

Revelation 22:12

Jesus is coming back. That is a fact, not fantasy. The question is – when? After Doug's death, I considered the end of times. I prayed about it, and I started paying closer attention to world events. A realization slowly came over me. Things happening in the world sounded very similar to what the Bible calls the "last days."

I started researching, knowing that every major crisis in the world could be wrongly associated with the end times. Each decade brought more and more people saying that Jesus' return was drawing near. When you bring up the fact that we may be living in the "last days" many people will comment "that is what they always say."

And that is true.

But some day one generation will be right.

Ironically, one of the signs of the last days is when people laugh about Jesus' return. *"First of all, you must understand that in the last days scoffers will come, scoffing and following their own evil desires. They will say, "Where is this 'coming' he promised?"*[1]

There are other signs that indicate we are living in the final days. Israel's rebirth as a nation is prophesied throughout the Bible and is one of the most amazing fulfillments in scripture.[2] It has been observed throughout history that once a race is removed from their homeland they cannot maintain their national identity for more than five generations.[3] Yet, the Jews have defied those odds for almost two thousand years.

In the last days, the prophet Zechariah says that Israel will be a stumbling block to all nations, and every nation of the world will be focused on the tiny state of Israel.[4] Today, the Middle East, the Israeli-Palestinian conflict, and the War on Terror makes the daily evening news.

Another significant sign is the increase in knowledge and transportation. Daniel 12:4 says the "time of the end" will be characterized by people going "here and there to increase knowledge." Today we are living in a world of movement, not only with air travel and space travel, but also with the Internet and webcams.

How long the end times last is another issue, but for sure, it doesn't last thousands of years. I would argue it doesn't even last hundreds of years. Jesus said, when you see the signs spoken of in the Bible, *"Lift up your heads, because your redemption is drawing near."*[5] Then He says something profound: *"I tell you the truth, this generation will certainly not pass away until all these things have happened."*[6]

What generation? The generation that sees all the signs taking place.

You need to make up your own mind whether or not we are living in the last days, but to understand my perspective, you need to realize that's what I believe. Why? "All these things" Jesus spoke of are happening now and they are happening faster than they have ever happened before.

But just like some of you, I questioned the signs, not because I didn't want them to be true, but because I did. I began to doubt my own thoughts. Was I taking what the Bible said and forming it into something I wanted? Or was I clearly understanding the world in light of scripture?[7]

Every time I opened my Bible there was another verse on "the end of days." In every Bible study I attended there was a comment about the "last days." In every song I listened to there was a hint of "thy kingdom come."

Prophecy of the last days started to surround me. I started to realize what I was seeing and believing was no coincidence.

During this time one verse gripped me. It reads, *"Prepare the way for the Lord; make straight in the wilderness a highway for our God. Every valley shall be raised up, every mountain and hill made low; the rough ground shall become level, the rugged places a plain. And the glory of the Lord will be revealed, and all mankind together will see it. For the mouth of the Lord has spoken."*[8]

"Prepare the way of the Lord," I kept repeating to myself over and over. "Prepare the way of the Lord."

I am no John the Baptist, who partially fulfilled this prophecy at Jesus' first coming, but I am a voice in the wilderness shouting, "Prepare the way of the Lord!"

After five years my beliefs haven't changed; they have only intensified as this world keeps fulfilling biblical prophecy. Years ago, I discovered a song called "Revival." It is by Robin Mark and he refers to Jesus' second coming as a train roaring in the distance. His exact words are, "I can hear that thunder in the distance, it's like a train on the edge of the town."[9]

It's like a train on the edge of the town.

Do you feel it? Can you feel the rumbling? Can you feel the Earth starting to shake?

He's coming back.

I played that song repeatedly when I first heard it. Then, only weeks after I discovered that song, I received another message from my God.

∽

My friend Roger and I helped lead the singing in the church I attended in Plymouth, New Hampshire. The church's computer was old and sometimes froze during worship, so Roger and I met at the church to see if my laptop would be better suited for Sunday services.

Roger plugged in my laptop and said, "I'm just going to pull up some music and try this out."

I started to tell him I didn't have any music on my laptop when he clicked the "Windows Media Player" icon on the screen.

"Sure you do," he replied.

I stared at the large projection screen that had a long list of music on it, stunned. I hadn't put any music on my laptop. I suddenly realized the list Roger was looking at was music Doug downloaded to our home computer to sync with his palm pilot before he deployed to Iraq. I purchased the laptop after Doug's death, when all my belongings were still on a barge across the ocean. Somehow the songs got transferred from my computer to my laptop.

"You have four hundred and fifty seven songs in here," Roger said, scrolling back and forth.

When Roger clicked on a random song to see if the system worked, my lips curved into a smile.

He had chosen the song, "Better Days."

It was the same title God had given me earlier, the song that assured me Doug loved me and he had never seen better days.

When the music started playing, it wasn't the "Better Days" I knew.

This "Better Days" was by Bruce Springsteen, Doug's favorite artist.[10] It was song number one hundred and fifty eight on the list. A random pick?

"Looks like it works," Roger said as he disconnected the system and the song was abruptly cut off.

After we wrapped up, I slid my computer in its case and hurriedly drove home. I knew in my gut Daddy had just sent me another message. I prayed I had the spiritual ears to hear it.

Better Days by Bruce Springsteen

Well my soul checked out missing as I sat listening
To the hours and minutes tickin' away
Yeah, just sittin' around waitin' for my life to begin
While it was all just slippin' away.
I'm tired of waitin' for tomorrow to come
Or that train to come roarin' 'round the bend
I got a new suit of clothes and a pretty red rose
And a woman I can call my friend

These are better days baby
Yeah there's better days shining through
These are better days baby
Better days with a girl like you

That was the first verse to the song, and with the way my mind had turned to of late I knew exactly what it meant.

Doug couldn't wait either. He couldn't wait for the train of our Lord and Savior to come. Jesus had dressed him in a new suit of clothes and he was holding a red rose with my name on it.

I sometimes thank my God for giving me a love story. It is a strange one, a unique one, but it is mine. And I love Him for it.

ↄ৩

Doug's eyes drifted to the scroll. He hadn't noticed it at first, the glory of God riveting his attention and freezing him where he knelt, but the Father held it tightly in His right hand. It had writing on both sides and was sealed with seven seals.

The voices of the creatures continued to sound: "Holy, Holy, Holy is the Lord God Almighty, who was, and is, and is to come!"[11] The tenor of their voices rumbled in Doug's chest like a coming train.

A lone angel flew overhead, its size twice that of the other angels. His face was stern, his chin set, and his hands were clinched with urgency. His hair shimmered with golden light and his eyes burned with blue flame. In a loud voice he proclaimed, "Who is worthy to break the seals and open the scroll?"[12]

The thunder grew louder and a thick bolt of lightning flashed overhead, illuminating the Ancient of Days with even more glory. Doug's eyes were drawn to the empty throne beside the Father. Where was Jesus?

The angel called again, this time in a tone so mournful it tore Doug's heart. "Who is worthy to break the seals and open the scroll?"

Doug began to weep, longing for the One who died for his soul. Although the heavens were filled with the redeemed and teeming with angels, there was a massive emptiness, a sudden helplessness as no one rose to the angel's challenge.

"Who is worthy to break the seals and open the scroll?"

Doug started to pray, almost overcome with despair. The redeemed around him did the same. Doug could hear their collective thought: *Come quickly, Lord Jesus!*

As if on cue, the four living creatures beside the throne paused in their unending song, and for a brief moment the air weighed heavy with silence.

Then Doug saw Him standing beside the Father. Blinding white diamonds seemed to tumble from His presence. The scars in His hands and feet drew the light and cast it back to the sky as scarlet jewels. The Son of Man stood beside the angels. His presence was all encompassing and never-ending. He was the Word, the Truth, and the Life.[13] He was everything. If Doug wasn't already on his knees he would be now. Jesus' presence demanded reverence.

The four living creatures unfurled their wings to the sky. Lifting their heads skyward they began to sing, "Worthy is the Lamb, who was slain, to receive power and wealth and wisdom and strength and honor and glory and praise!"[14]

The red stains in Jesus' hands brightened. The diamonds tumbling from His presence became the sun.

The Son of Man stepped forward and took the scroll.

It was the beginning of the end.

Excitement clinched Doug's chest as he heard his own voice merge with the rest of the redeemed. "All glory, praise and honor to the King!"[15]

Doug leaped to his feet and cheered, almost overcome with gratitude as his chest swelled with a feeling he could not define. It was more than exuberance, more than praise, joy didn't even come close to describing the sensation, and hope was far too past tense. It was now. It was here. It was everything. It was more.

"This is more. Jesus is more. More," Doug said as he fell to his knees beside the sea of glass. He felt a hand on his shoulder and turned to see Samson smiling with tears trailing down his rough, bearded cheeks. Daniel stood beside him, clasping his hands and rocking forward to his toes, radiant rays of praise beaming from his face.

"More," Samson said as he threw his head back and lifted his hands to the sky. "More!" he shouted, spinning and leaping in the crowd of saints, his massive frame weaving back and forth like an oak in a field of daisies. Then Doug was laughing and crying at the same time, praying and shouting with Samson, as God's unending, perfect light washed over him anew. Daniel stood beside Doug and together they watched Samson twirl. Doug could hear Daniel's whispered words of praise, "More, Father, more Father, more!"

Doug turned to the sea of glass as his tears continued to fall. "Wait, Beautiful. Jesus is coming, and when Jesus comes there will be more. There will be more!"

CHAPTER NINE
Under Enemy Attack

"Submit therefore to God. Resist the devil and he will flee from you. Draw near to God and He will draw near to you."

James 4:7-8a

Where was the enemy? I knew he was there, lurking in the shadows, waiting to pounce.

"Be self-controlled and alert. Your enemy the devil prowls around like a roaring lion looking for someone to devour. Resist him, standing firm in the faith."[1]

Over the course of the first year I knew God was protecting me, providing a shield around my heart. That is why, I believe, I felt such an urgency to discover the answers to my ultimate questions of "do I wait?"

The lion wanted in and he would do anything to destroy my faith. His teeth were bared, his claws were newly sharpened, and he was settling into attack stance three years after Doug's death.

The enemy prowls and lurks, ready to devour you when the slightest doubt enters your mind. Ironically, the attack I was expecting was far from the attack I received. I thought the enemy would assault my convictions about marriage, about my belief in the end times, and my beliefs about Heaven.

But the enemy doesn't waste time striking the one place a soldier has donned her greatest armor. I had a firm foundation in my convictions and this foundation was built by the master architect and builder.[2] Nothing can destroy Daddy's foundation, not even the enemy.

My breastplate was made of iron, and the devil knew he would waste his darts if he attacked my heart. So he went straight for my jugular, from where my faith stemmed.

I know now, more than I have ever known before, because of Daddy's grace, my prayerful friends, and my ceaseless inner pleas, Daddy sent His angels to surround me on May 25, 2006. Daddy's voice was so clear, so unclouded, God's wings shielded my heart from questions and doubts.

"He will cover you with his feathers, and under his wings you will find refuge; his faithfulness will be your shield and rampart."[3]

When I had passed through the waters, Daddy was right there, and when I had walked though the fire, He didn't let it harm me.[4] However, as time moved on Daddy decided He needed to sift something from me, so when the enemy asked Daddy nodded His consent.[5]

It started with one comment from a friend, but that comment was so devastating, so destructive, it affected my faith. The comment had nothing to do with Doug or with Heaven. It attacked my judgment.

When I was a little girl one of my Sunday school teachers gave me a bookmark with my name and its meaning written in pretty script. "Nicole" it said, "Victory of Faith." It quoted I John 5:4, *"For everyone born of God overcomes the world. This is the victory that has overcome the world, even our faith."*

Over the years I've looked at that bookmark and wondered if I would ever live up to my name, always focusing on the "victory" I could achieve while completely ignoring the element of faith needed to assure that victory.

Satan knows exactly what your name means, and he will attack it. So he bypassed every conviction I held about Heaven and went for my core, my strength, and the meaning of my name – my faith.

Someone questioned my judgment and so I started questioning my judgment, not only in substantial decisions, but also in minor choices.

Had I wandered from God's path? I feared I hadn't heard His voice correctly. After all, my judgment had been questioned. My judgment was suspect.

I put myself under a microscope. The decisions I had to make alone, those in which I had to rely on God to help me, became something feared. My judgment wasn't sound. How could I trust what I thought I had heard from God?

One doubt began to spiral into fear and fear began to spiral into panic. If someone questioned my opinion, even if it was about the sky being blue, my anxiety shot even higher.

As the Bible says, one doubt is all it takes to send you into a tailspin.

"He who doubts is like a wave of the sea, blown and tossed by the wind. That man should not think he will receive anything from the Lord; he is a double-minded man, unstable in all he does."[6]

Fear dominated my life. All because of one comment and my own insecurity. Daddy wanted it gone, so He sat back and waited.

Although He was still there, I didn't feel Him. Although He continued to guide me, I didn't realize it. I cried, I feared, and I questioned my Daddy and His love for me.

જ

Doug held his breath. In moments he and the saints would witness something untold millions had read about for thousands of years. The seals of Revelation had been debated over the centuries, and now it was time to break their mysteries.

When Doug felt a hand on his shoulder, he turned to Samson. The whimsical childlike gleam in his friend's eyes was gone, replaced with a fiercely protective warrior's gaze. For the first time Doug saw what the Philistines had feared for decades — a man who could kill a thousand men with a jawbone of a donkey.[7] Samson's eyes never drifted from Jesus as he tightened his grip on Doug's shoulder.

"The season is over. It's time to pray."

The urgency in that message sent with it a fiery passion inside Doug. With a surety he couldn't put to words, he knew.

Nic was under attack.

Then he felt it — doubt. It spiraled around him as if it wanted his own soul. If an emotion had color doubt would be black, ebony black, because it not only claimed your confidence, it stripped you of all joy. Nic had hope in their Savior's promises of a future kingdom; she had joy because she knew the world in which she lived was only a shadow of the world to come; she had answers to prayers and assurances from God, yet something had happened that caused her to doubt who she was and what God had told her she needed to do. Friends couldn't surround her constantly; parents could only reassure her so much. Nic had to grow accustomed to God's still, small voice and become confident in the decisions she made because of that voice. Ultimately, under God's sheltering wing and by His grace, she alone had to stand strong in her faith.

While the emotions swirled around him, Doug instantly knew why God was allowing this attack. Nic was strong, but she wasn't confident. Her faith ran deep, yet her personality caused her to swallow her opinion more than most.

She could whisper her beliefs to a close friend, but she didn't want to shout her beliefs from the mountaintop.

God was allowing her to go through this season because it would make her stronger. He needed to prepare her armor, and armor with doubt was no armor at all.

Doug could hear the first whispered words of the enemy.

"You are wrong!"

With that accusation, Nic's world began to spiral. The enemy had planted a seed and that seed has sprouted.

Nic began to sink, questioning not only who she was, but also whether or not she had made the right decisions. When she began questioning her decisions she began to question God.

As Doug's silent prayers lifted skyward he felt Nic's doubts began to grow. Her prior conviction drained and the fire that had consumed her nearly extinguished. Fear could do great damage. It could not only force you to question every decision, it could also cause you to question God's love.

"Be strong and courageous, Nic," Doug whispered. "Do not be afraid. Your Daddy is still with you."[8]

I tried to break free from the fear, but I could not. I prayed, I pleaded, and I begged. It did not cease. At times it faded; at other times it overwhelmed, but Daddy says He will never allow you to undergo anything without a reason. Romans 8:28 says, *"We know that in all things God works for the good of those who love him, who have been called according to his purpose."* Daddy was going to break this fear from me or the task He had assigned me would be unattainable.

I had to stand up. I had to be strong and stand firm in my convictions. That meant I had to answer any who might question me with a firm, yet loving, "No, you are wrong."

I am a peacemaker by nature, one who wants to please everyone. The thought of disappointing someone terrified me. Yet God said there was only one person I needed to please and I already pleased Him. I was His child, His daughter, and He loved me enough to sift out what needed sifting. Daddy knows best.

I needed to be right in His eyes and His eyes alone. I couldn't rely on others to validate my convictions. Most scholars would vehemently disagree with my conclusions. Close friends would question. Family would doubt. I had to stand firm on Daddy's messages and be sure of my faith.

Daddy was teaching me how to stop questioning and to believe even more deeply than I had before. It took a lot of growing, a lot of praying and a lot of thinking, but in the end my focus sharpened, my spirit deepened and my convictions only grew stronger.

Daddy knew the fear had to go. I have an assignment to complete. It begins with this book.

Satan tried to take my faith with an IED on May 25, 2006. He can't have it. I know the truth.

Daddy wants me to tell you the truth.

Jesus is coming back.

The millennial reign of Christ is about to become a reality. Its purpose is to right all the wrongs that have happened to God's people.

This life is not the final chapter.

Satan wants us to believe this is all we have; don't let him convince you.

If you lose your life here, you will gain it there, and there is far greater than here.

One day soon there will be a blast of the trumpet. The dead in Christ will rise and the believing faithful will also be taken.

When I hear that trumpet sound I will see my Doug again.

When I hear that trumpet sound I will be able to bow at my Savior's feet.

When I hear that trumpet sound I will crawl into my Daddy's lap.

What will happen when you hear the trumpet sound?

Will you be taken? Or will you be left?

He is coming back.

He is coming soon.

Are you ready?

A FUTURE CHAPTER...
The Opening of the Seals

"So do not throw away your confidence; it will be richly rewarded. You need to persevere so that when you have done the will of God, you will receive what he has promised. For in just a very little while, 'He who is coming will come and will not delay. But my righteous one will live by faith. And if he shrinks back, I will not be pleased with him.' But we are not of those who shrink back and are destroyed, but of those who believe and are saved."

Hebrews 10:35-39

Doug thought back to when Nic had read to him the differing views of the book of Revelation. Now, as the creatures' song reached a crescendo, the time was upon them, and it was very clear what was about to transpire. Prevailing Christian thought placed the rapture before the rise of the Antichrist but that was not what scripture taught.

The saints on Earth would see the rise of the son of destruction and they would be present for his persecution.[1]

Doug sent a silent prayer of thanks to his Father and lifted his hands skyward in honor of his Savior. Nic had victory over her doubts and she once again turned her thoughts to the coming King. The anticipation he had first felt at the sea of glass came rushing back.

Almost time.

The voice of many angels, thousands upon thousands of angels, merged with the cry of the creatures and the voices of the saints, "Worthy is the Lamb, who was slain, to receive power and wealth and wisdom and strength and honor and glory and praise!"[2]

The elect surrounding him were still, all eyes riveted on the King. Jesus hadn't made a move to open the scroll but as He stood there His glory intensified like an image in a computer that had been enhanced a hundredfold. A mere glance at the King of Kings would bring the enemy to his knees.

The creatures surrounding the throne lifted skyward, all six wings unfurled, spinning in glorious unison, "Worthy is the Lamb, who was slain, to receive power and wealth and wisdom and strength and honor and glory and praise!"[2]

The Son of Man stepped forward. As His finger moved to break the first seal, Doug heard the clip of horses hooves pounding the ground with resolution, distant at first, but becoming louder and more insistent until their echo rumbled in Doug's spirit and cast a chill over the saints as they watched the first seal break.[3]

Doug held his breath as he turned his gaze to the Earth. Although he knew what he would see, the mere sight of the first horseman of the Apocalypse made his insides shudder. The rider's eyes betrayed his true beliefs. Those eyes would convince the world of hope, yet dash those hopes like pieces of pottery. This man would mock the Most High and persecute the saints with vast arrogance.[4]

The rider held a bow but it had no arrows, symbolic of the Antichrist's rise to power by deception alone. But a crown graced his head, indicating his success.

This man would be Satan's minion on Earth; he would offer peace to Israel and hope and prosperity to the world, yet inwardly he knew he would betray his own words in time.

Most of the Earth would believe his lies. Many would turn away from the faith because of him and many more would put their trust in his deceptions.

Many in the Islamic world would herald him as savior. When they did, the terrorists would unite to terrorize the world. Some formally moderate Muslims would become radical. With their savior in control, they would believe nothing could stop them from spreading Islam over the entire globe. Their goal would be world domination.[5]

But the true King of Kings would ultimately destroy that false hope.

Doug breathed in a special thanks to his Creator. Nic was looking up. She knew what was to come and she would tell others.

"Come," the Earth said.

"Come," the saints said.

"Come," Nic said.

"Come quickly Lord Jesus," Doug said.

He could almost feel the Earth shiver.

He wondered if Nic could feel the approaching rider. "The train has started, Nic." Doug said. "Be strong."

&

At times we question if God loves us. I can't imagine how much that hurts Him, the one who sacrificed everything for us. We wonder why and absolutely fear the next time pain will come our way. But never forget the fact that God loves you. He loves me and He loves Doug. But the questions still remain don't they? If He loves us, how could He allow this? Because if God is who He says He is, He could have stopped the IED. He could have influenced Doug to take a different road. Let's cut to the chase – God could have stopped my pain from ever coming to fruition.

Well, there're some things we will never understand in this life, but I do know one thing: Doug's life was never in question. When his life ended here, it didn't truly end; it just continued in a different place.

Christ didn't come to this Earth to suffer and die so that we could have a long, happy life here. He came to guarantee we would live with Him forever. He came so that no matter what happens, nothing can truly harm us.

"For I am convinced that neither death nor life, neither angels nor demons, neither the present nor the future, nor any powers, neither height nor depth, nor anything else in all creation, will be able to separate us from the love of God that is in Christ Jesus our Lord."[6]

God can see the present and He can see the future. He can see the moment Doug and I are reunited. Oh, can you imagine the rejoicing! Daddy is like a parent on Christmas Eve waiting in expectation as His children wake and rush into the living room. He wants to give us that joy more than anything. He wants to surprise us with blessings and crown us with crowns. Can you imagine the day!

&

Doug watched as his Savior broke the second seal.[7] The horse's hooves were louder than the first; so loud in fact, Doug instinctively took a step back. The rider on the red horse held a large sword. Blood already dripped from its tip as he barreled over the Earth stirring chaos in his wake. Men would slay each

other because of the spirit of the rider and peace would flee with his passing. Doug continued to whisper his prayers, not only for Nic, but also for
all those who would come in contact with the second horseman. Many saw
the Antichrist as a conquering hero, and because of that, the second rider was
now unleashed.

Terrorists began to usher in what they thought would bring about total
dominion of the Earth, and in doing so they thought they were offering a service to their god.[8]

Doug watched the second rider blaze across the Earth. He could almost
hear the screams of panic as the terrorist's sword rose across the land.

"Stand firm, Nic," Doug whispered. "You are the warrior now."

༃

There is one more thing I believe. If Doug's death would guarantee just one
additional person to accept Jesus' sacrifice, maybe, just maybe, we have found
hope in the midst of tragedy.

One time I was asking about Doug's death and the reason behind it. I said
something to God that seems a little cruel when I write it on paper. I said, "I
can understand you allowing Doug's death if ten people come to faith in you
because of this, but one? I can't accept that. Please, just let there be ten that
learn to love you because of this!"

I heard, "How about a hundred," in my head.

I don't know if that meant one hundred people or a lot more than ten, but I
pray there will be a lot of people who decide to live their lives for God because
of Doug's testimony.

At times it seems I'm between Earth and Heaven, trying to figure out the
madness of it all. Many things in this world don't make sense, but when you
think about them in light of eternity, through God's eyes and not your own,
peering through the Word as you study the happenings around you, in a crazy
way, it slowly starts to come together.

The Bible is an amazing book. You can read it, know it, even memorize it,
yet when certain things happen and you look at a scripture you've read a thousand times before it becomes not something different, but something more. It's
like seeing a rock halfway in the ground and pulling it out only to discover it
has endless sides.

At times I am sitting in my house and Heaven is right above me, ready to descend. But when I am in the world, in the madness, I can't seem to see the first sign of it. Only when I put on my armor and don my sword do I walk into the world and see it as it should be seen.[9] I have had contact with a few other surviving spouses. I always tell them the same thing, "Hold on tight to what God is telling you. When you walk into the world it will try to take God's promises away from you. Don't let it. Hold on tight and believe."

"Do not store up for yourselves treasures on earth, where moth and rust destroy, and where thieves break in and steal. But store up for yourselves treasures in heaven, where moth and rust do not destroy, and where thieves do not break in and steal."[10]

I never understood that verse until May 25, 2006. Now my greatest treasure is in Heaven. I'm not letting go. I'm holding on tight to the promises of my Savior.

૭౧

Doug and the saints remained rooted to the sea of glass, watching the events foretold centuries ago continue to unfold.

The war was waging and it looked like the tides of evil were winning. Doug knew better. The saints had begun to shine like the stars as their fiery trial continued to refine their faith.[11] It was something to behold. In Heaven you could gaze down on the saints on Earth and see dots of brilliant light moving around like fireflies in the night. Yet, you could also see them individually, as if you were watching a million movies at once. Some movies were farther away and some were closer. Nic's movie played out right before him. He could watch the slow transformation of her character as if he were standing right before her. The movies were moving faster now.

Almost time.

Doug watched as his Savior broke the third and fourth seal in quick succession.[12] He felt his body stiffen as he turned his gaze to the Earth.

The third rider was mounted on an ebony black horse, holding a pair of scales in his hand. He moved far more quickly than the other two riders.

The creatures surrounding the throne of God suddenly unfurled their wings and with a mournful cry shouted, "A quart of wheat for a day's wages, and three quarts of barley for a day's wages, and do not damage the oil and the wine!"[13]

The rise of the Antichrist and then the subsequent violence of the second rider ushered in the third.

The famine would be widespread and catastrophic to many families, but it wouldn't be so severe to stop the daily sacrifice in the newly built Jewish temple.[13] The oil and wine would continue to be poured out, symbolic of the Holy Spirit's continued presence on Earth and the atoning blood of the Savior who could cover the repentant of their sins. The spirit was still accessible and the blood was still available for unbelievers to be cleansed. Those on the Earth could still turn to the Way, the Truth and the Life.[14]

The saints surrounding him were silent, everyone watching the scene below. Doug could hear the cry of the elect on Earth, *"Come quickly, Lord Jesus!"*

The rider on the pale horse followed in the black rider's wake. The rider's name was Death, and Hades followed close behind, leaving a blackness so vast it hurt.

As Death passed, Doug heard the screams of those on the Earth who would meet him. When people looked into the rider's eyes they wouldn't survive. Doug whispered a heartfelt prayer for the saints on Earth.

A quarter of the Earth would fall due to the sword, famine and plague of the riders. Many would turn from the faith because of their severity. Only the true saints would remain pure to the end. Others, those dead in faith, those lukewarm in spirit, those complacent in their service, would falter in their walk. Only those who were running the race set before them had read the signs of the times and prepared.[15]

Doug bowed to his knees and began to pray because of the fourth way in which those on Earth were to be killed.

By the beasts of the earth.[16]

The mark of the beast had been introduced. The Antichrist would now usher in the persecution of the faithful and aim for the destruction of Israel.[17]

"Two more seals to go, Nic. Then there will be more. Then there will be more!"

৶

When something happens that takes the wind from your lungs you never know how to respond to the question, "How are you?"

Most everyone uses those words as a greeting. They slip from innocent lips like butter. It is the fabric of our society.

"How are you?"

Although innocent and genuine, I never know how to answer that question. People were posing it to me mere weeks after Doug was killed. Years later, I still don't know quite how to reply.

Most of the time I say, "Making it." If I am feeling humorous I say, "Joyfully sucky."

Joyfully sucky about sums it up. I'm not happy. How can I be when half of me is gone?[18] But I am joyful because of Jesus. He came and He conquered. He paid the price for Doug's sin and He paid the price for mine. Nothing, not even an IED on the terrorist ridden streets of Bagdad could undo what Jesus did on the cross.

"My sheep listen to my voice; I know them, and they follow me. I give them eternal life, and they shall never perish; no one can snatch them out of my hand."[19]

My third response for "How are you doing?" has never been taken well. When I am feeling spunky I say, "Waiting for the rapture."

That sends the recipients of my reply into a tailspin. After the moments it takes to register what I mean there is awkward silence.

The world has its unspoken rules and one of those rules is, "you have to be happy here." Most people fall into the trap of depending on certain pleasures or possessions to enjoy life more.

It's a lie. There is nothing that will make you happier. The more you get, the more you want.

God says, *"Seek first his kingdom and his righteousness."*[20] When you follow this advice, this world fades in comparison to the world awaiting us.

"Waiting for the rapture" is really the way I feel. It isn't sad; it is hopeful. And that hope is in God. For those who believe, God's promises stand firm.

What are His promises? I'm glad you asked.

God will always be with us.

"I will not in any way fail you nor give you up nor leave you without support, I will not, I will not, I will not in any degree leave you helpless nor forsake you nor let you down (relax my hold on you)! Assuredly not!"[21]

God will always hear us.

"I call on you, Oh God, for you will answer me; give ear to me and hear my prayer."[22]

God will ultimately save us.

"In that day they will say, 'Surely this is our God; we trusted in him, and he saved us. This is the Lord, we trusted in him; let us rejoice and be glad in his salvation.'"[23]

And there will be no more agony.

"He will swallow up death forever. The Sovereign Lord will wipe away the tears from all faces; he will remove the disgrace of his people from all the earth. The Lord has spoken."[24]

We will live forever with Him.

"For my Father's will is that everyone who looks to the Son and believes in him shall have eternal life, and I will raise him up at the last day."[25]

Because of God's grace, I am able to stand. Because of God's love, I am able to breathe. Because of God's promises I am able to put one foot in front of the other and look forward to the day when evil will be defeated forever and I can once again hold Doug's hand.

∽

As his Savior opened the fifth seal, Doug knew what he had to do. He spun from the sea of glass and made his way through the saints. Samson caught up to him with a questioning look.

"I have to get something for Nic."

"But the seals," Samson said, looking over his shoulder at Jesus.

Jesus turned Doug's way. There was a knowing smile on His face and His eyes held the compassion of billions. The light spilling from His countenance reached out to Doug, urging him forward, and although Doug didn't see Jesus' lips move he heard a firm, yet gentle, "Go" in his head.

Samson sensed Jesus' silent command and instantly relaxed. "I will meet you beside the Savior," he said. "It would be an honor to descend together."

Doug didn't quite know what Samson meant, but he decided to dwell on it later. As his Savior broke the fifth seal, Doug ran from the sea of glass, intent on his aim. He knew without a shadow of a doubt what he must do and why he had to do it. The task would complete the circle of faith. Nic was not fully aware of how much the saints in Heaven followed those on Earth. She was unsure if the messages being sent from her Daddy also came from him.

But their Father was a romantic. He had fashioned Eve to fit Adam in the beginning and He was fashioning the bride of Christ to fit His Son in the end. As the Bible said, love never dies and many waters cannot overcome it.[26]

Doug urged his feet faster, pushing harder than he had ever run before. He strained his muscles without weariness; he breathed in the air of his God without fear of failure. He ran so fast it felt as if he were running on air. He couldn't even feel the ground beneath his feet. The sights surrounding him were a marvelous blur of color and light. In front of him was the gate to the New Jerusalem with the angel standing guard. As Doug ran through the gate the creature laughed with joy. "Go, Doug of the Savior! It's almost time for the reunion!" The angel's laughter continued to follow him, causing Doug's lips to curve into a crooked smile.

The reunion.

When Doug finally stopped before Nic's home, he almost couldn't believe his eyes. For in the skies surrounding it, as far as the eye could see, were angels lifting houses on their backs and flying toward the New Jerusalem with breathtaking speed. There were too many to count.

Tears came to Doug's eyes as he lifted his hands skyward. No amount of persecution could claim the elect. The Antichrist could kill their bodies, but he could never snatch their souls from the Savior's hand.[27]

Doug continued to watch in wonder as what appeared to be an entire city drifted past. He felt Nic's unease as those she knew were taken and killed. In the distance another angel lifted a home off the ground. Doug could hear the martyrs cry in his gut, resonating in his spirit and sending a shiver through his being.

"How long, Sovereign Lord, holy and true, until you judge the inhabitants of the earth and avenge our blood?"[28]

The Antichrist wouldn't share his kingdom with anyone. Christians standing firm in their faith were being taken by the thousands. If they didn't convert to the Antichrist ideology, they were killed. It was as simple as that.

"One more seal," Doug whispered as he stepped closer to Nic's house. The angel laying the stones was much higher now. Only a few more stones to place and Nic's house would be complete.

He knew what he was looking for and spotted it instantly. Nestled between the flawless diamonds and the opaque stones, the red rose had grown larger and only added to the beauty of the place. Even fully grown, the rose held no thorns. It was a flawless rose, not only in color and shape, but also in construction. Jesus had fashioned it for Nic with the sole purpose of Doug retrieving it from here before the rapture.

The air surrounding Doug grew thick, urging him to hurry. Doug broke the rose off the vine and stepped back to look up at the darkening sky. Although God's eternal light still eclipsed this place, he could tell the cosmos was preparing for the sixth seal. The angel stopped his work and looked down at Doug with a widening grin.

"Watch."

With the angel's words Doug's breath caught, for from out of every crevice of stone vines started to grow and before Doug's eyes roses sprang, lighting every flawless diamond with a deep, rich red. Whenever Nic looked at the walls of her home she would be reminded of her Daddy's faithfulness, her Savior's provision, and the love she wouldn't release.

The angel descended to the ground and stood at attention beside Nic's home, a glorious smile lighting his face. When Doug looked around the field of houses he saw the other angelic workers doing the same. The bride of Christ had made herself ready. The heavenly preparations were complete.

Doug looked at the darkening sky, a small smile spreading across his face as he thought about the reunion.

Doug perused the angels' faces that now stood beside each dwelling. They were waiting for the sound of the ram's horn; with that cry the houses of those remaining saints would be ushered into the New Jerusalem. Those believers still on Earth would never die. They would be lifted from the Earth to meet their Lord in the air.[29]

Doug spun as he remembered the vision he first had when he came to this place: an earthquake, a dark sun, a red moon; the blast of the shofar, Nic's joyful cry, his urn toppling, ashes bursting skyward; a white horse, a red rose and an embrace.

Then laughter, more glorious laughter than he had ever heard before.

Doug started to run back to the city of his God, back to Jesus, and back to the end, for it was really just beginning.

ॐ

We all have our mountains to climb and this one is mine. No matter what you are going through, no matter what your mountain is, trust Daddy. He will take what Satan intended for harm and use it for glory.[30] Stand on the rock of Jesus and don't relax your grip on Daddy's hand. You better believe He won't let go of yours.[31] The solid foundation of Jesus' sacrifice will never fail you. And if you choose to believe, those waters, those rivers, and that fire, won't harm you. You have the Holy One of Israel by your side.[32]

"Be strong and courageous. Do not be terrified; do not be discouraged, for the Lord your God will be with you wherever you go."[33]

He will. He has been with me every step of the way. He has answered my prayers and has given me the strength and insight to respond to His voice.

So today? Where am I?

"I press on toward the goal to win the prize for which God has called me heavenward in Christ Jesus."[34]

Jesus is coming soon. Heaven is descending. The Millennium will be ushered in, and my duty - ?

"Let love and faithfulness never leave you; bind them around your neck, write them on the tablet of your heart. Then you will win favor and a good name in the sight of God and man."[35]

Some people might look at me and wonder how I can love God after what He allowed to happen, but how can I not love Him even more for what He is going to do?

I can't imagine loving God any more than I do now. I sometimes wonder if things happen in this life so you will love God to the fullest. I don't know, but I do know nothing in this world could make me love Him more. Because one day I will be able to take Doug's face in my hands, look into his eyes and tell him how much I missed him. My God can put him back together again. That broken body that is now ashes, that was delivered in three urns, can be made whole again. Not a different Doug, not one that is recreated, one that is reformed. Those ashes, my Doug's ashes, will one day take to the sky.

"For the Lord himself will come down from heaven, with a loud command, with the voice of the archangel and with the trumpet call of God, and the dead in Christ will rise first. After that, we who are still alive and are left will be caught up together with them in the clouds to meet the Lord in the air. And so we will be with the Lord forever. Therefore, encourage each other with these words."[36]

I have decided not to scatter any of Doug's ashes because when my Jesus comes back and those trumpets sound, I want to run into my bedroom and watch those ashes burst to the sky. I want to see it with my own eyes. I want to see the glory of my God.

I have often thought about falling to my knees before Jesus and taking His feet in my hands. I can imagine seeing the nail scars as tears drip from my chin. And the first thing I will say?

"Thank you so much, Jesus. Thank you so much for saving my Doug." You think this world is great? Wait until the next one. He's coming back. Amen and amen. Come quickly, Lord Jesus.

A FUTURE CHAPTER. . .

The Sixth Seal

"The sun will be turned to darkness and the moon to blood before the coming of the great and dreadful day of the Lord. And everyone who calls on the name of the Lord will be saved."

Joel 2:31-32a

The saints were no longer surrounding the sea of glass; they were on the crystal expanse. As soon as Doug joined them his body changed.

He no longer had his temporary dwelling. He was once again the spirit the angels had ushered into Heaven on May 25, 2006. Although he could still feel and see the form of his body he could also sense a yearning for completeness, a sense of knowing there was something more.

Samson stepped beside him and although he still looked like the man Doug knew, he was not. It was as if Samson had stripped himself of all vibrant colors and replaced them with pastels.

"I was hoping we could descend together," Samson said with his childlike grin. "I look forward to meeting Nic. Soon she will have the more she has been searching for, that we all have been searching for."

Doug smiled, overwhelmed by the thought. Then a joy surfaced, far surpassing any joy he had ever felt before. It was as if every molecule of his being screamed it, knew it, and became it. That was it. He was joy.

The saints parted as Jesus moved forward, gliding over the sea of glass with eyes of blazing fire. He held a man in His arms. The man's face was broken, bruised and bleeding, yet as he opened his eyes and looked at his Savior an indescribable beauty radiated from him. Doug knew his story as if he had lived it himself. Captured at the heart of the Antichrist's empire, the man had been

beaten unmercifully by soldiers for not yielding his faith or his soul. He had
denied the mark of the beast and had paid dearly for it.[1]

As the saints looked on, the man's skin smoothed, his eyes brightened and
his wounds healed. Tears rolled down his unblemished face as sobs of joy shivered through his body. Crowns of gold and silver, dotted with precious stones,
appeared on his head - the faithful reward of the martyr.

Jesus reached out one hand and wiped the tears from the man's eyes.

"Well done!"

The saints surrounding the sea cheered, and it was a cry so powerful, so
beautiful, that Doug fell to his knees, overcome with gratitude. The merged
voices of the saints came together, praising the Savior and honoring the sacrifice
of the final martyr of the Earth.

Jesus stopped in the middle of the sea and stood the man to his feet as the
air surrounding them started to shake. It felt as if the sea of glass was an ocean
angered by the winds, yet Doug knew it wasn't the sea of glass itself that was in
turmoil, but the Earth beneath.

Jesus lifted the scroll into the air and broke the sixth seal.

Below him, the shaking intensified. The Earth reeled to and fro like a
drunkard.[2] The sun turned black and the moon to blood giving the saints on
Earth the final sign of their sudden disappearance – the rapture – when their
Savior would shout a command to meet Him in the clouds.[3]

And then Doug fell. It was so quick, so complete, that he couldn't see anything. He felt the Savior with him and the saints surrounding him, yet he knew
if he tried to reach out and touch them he would find himself alone. But he was
never truly alone was he? Jesus always went with him and before him.[4] There was
nothing to fear as the scene surrounding him faded. Jesus was there, and Jesus
was in complete control.

Then as soon as Doug thought he would be able to define what was happening, he felt different.

He was in something.

Whatever he entered was in upheaval. He could hear the violent shaking of
rock and stone. He could hear the rumble and rolling of the land. He was on
Earth again and it was in chaos. It was the beginning of the Lord's fury due to
the death of His saints and the persecution of His nation Israel.

As the ram's horn echoed across the land, Doug felt himself falling, yet
this time it was a physical fall, not a spiritual descent. A loud crack sounded
and shook him violently but not as much as the trumpet's blast. The cry of

the ram's horn was everywhere. Doug not only felt the cry in his ears, but also in every pore. It called him, and then he felt himself, his old self, become so much more.

"Behold the bridegroom comes!"[5] The voice of the archangel resonated in the air, spilling joy with every syllable. Doug heard shouts and weeping but he couldn't yet open his eyes.

Then there was light. It spilled inside him, flooding him with the promise of a new day, and when his vision cleared he saw Nic running toward him.

Tears coursed down her cheeks as she found his eyes. But the smile that lit her face dominated her features and carried with it a warmth greater than the brightest sun.

She called his name but he couldn't respond. That more feeling had settled inside him again, and instead of being just more, it was everything.

Doug reached out his hand as he started to ascend to the call of his Savior. He couldn't stop his body's response to the Lord's command any more than a waterfall could stop its tumbling. Every molecule in his body was answering the trumpet blast, responding to its summons. His life hadn't even begun to begin. This was his birth, a new birth, and a new life.

Then Nic began to change. The fine wrinkles in her face smoothed, the pain in her eyes lifted, and her skin transformed from mere dust to rays of light. As she clasped his hand her eyes reflected his feelings.

More. More than more. Everything.

The trails of Nic's tears seemed out of place on her radiant face. He wanted to wipe them away but he knew it wasn't his place anymore. He was not enough. Although they loved each other completely, he was not, nor had he ever been, enough. Only his Father or his Savior could erase those tears. Only Nic's Daddy or her Jesus.[6]

Nic seemed to know that too because her smile lifted even higher as her tears continued to fall. Doug wanted to say something but there were no words to describe what he was now feeling. Nic's arm encircled his neck as they soared toward the heavens, spinning in the cosmos.

Then the sound of Nic's laughter, her glorious laughter, rose skyward toward the fast approaching light.

As they spun and twirled, Doug saw others all around him doing the same, laughing and twirling, spinning and shouting, "Great and marvelous are your deeds, Lord God Almighty. Just and true are your ways, King of the ages. Who will not fear you, O Lord, and bring glory to your name?"[7]

The stars began to fall around them, like a glorious display of fireworks, but Doug instinctively knew the universe was now in chaos. The wrath of God had begun.[8]

It was necessary. Jesus was about to return to judge the world. Those left behind needed to repent — and quickly. God was urging them to believe and have life in the Lamb.

As the welcoming light of the King engulfed them, Nic quickly released him, dropped to her knees, and gripped her Savior's feet. Doug didn't have to hear Nic's words to know what she said. As her body was racked with sobs, Jesus reached down, drew her to himself, and gently wiped away her tears.

Doug had never seen anything more beautiful in his life.

The End. . .
Or the Beginning

"Then the Lord my God will come, and all the holy ones with him. On that day there will be no light, no cold or frost. It will be a unique day, without daytime or nighttime — a day known to the Lord. When evening comes, there will be light."

Zechariah 14:5b-7

The air was thick with anticipation. The saints were mounted on white horses and lined up on Doug's right and left. The silence was so silent it shouted. Before him, the commander of the army sat motionless on His white steed. Many crowns set atop the rider's head and His eyes were a blazing furnace as He peered down upon the Earth, a righteous judge to the events transpiring there.[1]

The horseman of the Apocalypse had tread across the land, causing chaos and unrest. The trumpets had laid the Earth's surface waste and uprooted those disloyal to the kingdom of the Lamb.[2] But the bowl judgments were the final reckoning.[3] Not only would they judge mankind, they would also herald the coming of the true King of Kings and usher in the final confrontation — the battle of Armageddon.

An angel flew overhead, the fifth since the commander told the troops to mount for battle, carrying a bowl in his hands.

The angel cried, "Darkness will cover the Earth and deep darkness the peoples; but the Lord will rise upon you, and His glory will appear upon you!"[4]

As the angel poured out his bowl, a dark shadow began to seep over the cosmos, like a curtain closing. Doug thought it appropriate. The old Earth was about to be made new. The first act was over. The second act was about to begin.

The Lamb lifted His arms. The robe drifted to His elbows, revealing nail-scarred hands. Doug never grew tired of seeing his Savior's scars. They were beauty beyond words. While the saints had been waiting in Heaven for the final stage of God's wrath, Doug had touched those scars. They even felt beautiful. He could still feel the rough texture of the nail bites. He could also feel Jesus hand on his shoulder and his Savior's breath against his forehead.

"You were worth it."

Doug shivered.

As the Earth was plunged into darkness, Jesus' brilliance seemed to multiply. His first coming was in a lowly manger, not so His second. Every man on Earth would see His majesty. The Son's light would encompass the world and His justice would consume the sinner. The Word, the true revelation, was about to descend.

The Earth quaked, the heavens trembled, and the sun's light faded from memory as Jesus moved forward. The Lord uttered His voice before His army. It was like a coming train.

The Antichrist and his kingdom would now see the shiny light of the Lion of the Tribe of Judah descending on them, yet they would still choose to fight the Almighty God.[5]

The creatures in the New Jerusalem slowly started singing. Their song drifted on the wind like a gentle mist of cleansing dew.

"Hallelujah! For our Lord God Almighty reigns. Let us rejoice and be glad and give him glory! For the wedding of the Lamb as come, and His bride has made herself ready! Hallelujah."[6]

The battle was about to begin. But Doug knew it wouldn't be much of a battle at all. Their commander had never been defeated and their enemy had never boasted any victories.

Doug's entire being tingled with joy as Nic tightened her grip around his waist. Doug glanced down at Nic's hands as she twirled a rose, a ruby red rose, formed from the pain of his passing and blossoming with the promise of their reunion.

This rose held no thorns, only beauty. This rose promised no more pain or separation. It was perfection, grown by the Lamb and given to him to bestow to the one it was meant for.

Doug's mouth lifted in a smile as he watched the Lamb move forward.

Doug placed his hand over Nic's. It was time to reclaim the Earth.

Then life could truly begin.

"Now faith is being sure of what we hope for and certain of
what we do not see." Hebrews 11:1

To the Reader:

I pray these words have brought you hope. I trust these words have made you realize what a loving Daddy we all have. I also hope this book has sparked a desire in you to know more about the return of the King.

I could have made this book a lot longer and tried to explain everything I believe in greater detail; however, I wanted to keep this story as simple as possible. This is my story, and I pray you understand and appreciate these words for what they are to me.

With that said, I do realize this story will bring many questions. I also realize this book will bring much discussion on my theological view. I ask each and every one of the biblical scholars reading this book to hear the underlying message of my words and not focus on where or when I place the rapture or how I feel about Heaven. Let this book be about hope. Let this book be about Daddy. Allow this book to be about the return of the King.

I am currently working on a commentary on the book of Revelation. If you would like to dig deeper into God's word or hear my thoughts on the end of days, the questions this book has sparked might be answered there. But don't wait for me. Open up the Word and pray to Daddy.

You too can have revelation.

And revelations can change your life.

Go, seek, and find the King. He is the revelation!

Amen and Amen! Come quickly, Lord Jesus!

Nic

A Special Thanks To My Battalion

"The sweet smell of incense can make you feel good, but true friendship is better still."

Proverbs 27:9 (CEV)

I don't think I would be standing today without the friends and family God so graciously put into my life. Their prayers and presence are what helps me stand firm. People all over the world were praying for me within minutes of the news. After I called our parents, I made another phone call. I called Amanda.

I met Amanda in Columbus, Georgia after Doug's tour in Alaska. Neither Doug nor I assumed we would make any lasting friendships in Columbus. After all, we were there for less than a year. We were wrong.

The first day we attended the church across from our home, Nathan and Rachel befriended us and invited us to their Bible study where we met Amanda and her husband Brad. Amanda and I quickly started spending the days together. Amanda is a rare friend. She instantly puts you at ease with her outgoing personality, yet when you need to talk she can curl up on the couch and listen without interruption.

Doug and I fell in love with the Bible study group we affectionately referred to as "the gang." They were Christians strong in the faith that didn't put on any masks and celebrated each other's differences.

When we left Georgia I was devastated. I didn't want to lose the friends I had come to adore. Doug and I had never found a group this strong, nor friendships this unbreakable. Looking back, God knew I would need an army surrounding me when the soldiers knocked on my door and the "Georgia gang" was tactical unit number one.

When I called Amanda to tell her about Doug I think some of my only words to her were "call the gang and tell them to pray."

She did. I think she had the entire city of Columbus on high alert. From there the message went across the nation. To this day, I still run into people in Georgia that look at me and say, "I have been praying for you for years."

If that isn't God at work I don't know what is.

God also knew tactical unit number one was only part of the battalion I would need. With plans to increase my circle of faith filled friends, God sent us to Heidelberg, Germany. Doug would be stationed there a year before taking command of a company. Again, a short time to make lifelong friendships, but a week after we arrived, Scott and Rachelle moved in upstairs. Rachelle and I instantly started tackling German shopping areas. We were a flurry of activity and laughter as we perused the stores. When people saw us together they thought we were sisters. During that year, it is what we became.

Before both of our husbands deployed, Rachelle and I talked about the "what if" scenarios, each terrified of the decisions we would have to make if the "worst" happened. There were talks of where we would live and where we would ultimately settle. Rachelle remembers me telling her I would go to New Hampshire until I could figure things out. It was a huge blessing to hear my own words of affirmation when I thought about staying in New Hampshire. But I always ended the conversation by telling her how blessed I was that I had met "the gang" in Georgia. I knew I would always have a place to ultimately return.

Rachelle became tactical unit number two.

Then Doug was transferred to Baumholder, Germany. Again, I didn't want to leave. Rachelle and I had formed an impenetrable bond, and I ultimately knew Doug would leave for Iraq six months after he took command.

When we arrived in Baumholder, suddenly and miraculously, God provided more friends, strong in the faith, that would be a unanimous shield of protection on May 25, 2006. First I met Jessica, who graciously volunteered to help me with the Family Readiness Group. We were on the phone constantly trying to formulate the best strategy to help the women while their husbands were away.

Then Jan moved in, freshly married and a ball of energy. Tara came next, a solid rock of faith, yet constantly on the move with thoughts coming in from every direction.

Then came Monica and Erica, Kristine and Paige, Joanna and Karen, Kim and Erin.

Tactical unit number three had formed.

When the soldiers came to notify me, Caleb was walking by. He alerted the girls in the complex and called his wife Erica, who was visiting family in the states. Jan and Tara were instantly by my side, standing firm when I could not. Although Jessica didn't live in the complex, she arrived as soon as she was able. Erica even cut her stateside trip short and flew back to help in any way she could.

Tactical unit number three was on high alert, tactical unit number two was on her way, and tactical unit number one was on their knees.

Rachelle knocked on my door late the night after Doug's death. There were no words to describe how relieved I was to see her. Although the girls in Birkenfeld were my shield they had only met Doug in passing. Rachelle had known Doug for a year. We had eaten many-a-dinner together, conducted a Bible study together, and had taken trips together. She had helped celebrate Dak's birth and had been there for me during Doug's long hours away from home.

Then my parents, tactical unit number four, arrived and took over worrying about what would happen next, where I would go, and assured me they were there for me no matter what.

Before I boarded the plane that would take me back to America, all of my closest friends in Germany asked me the same question, "Do you want me to come to the services in Plymouth?" To each of them I replied, "No, come after the services, when I will be alone. I will need you more then."

Besides, I knew once I landed in New Hampshire tactical unit number one would be on its way.

༄

I will never forget the flag. When I arrived at Doug's services at Plymouth Regional High School it hung beautifully suspended between the raised ladders of two fire trucks. It was quite possibly the largest flag I have ever seen. It was a dreary day, the air heavy with rain. Hoards of people filed past the flag and filled the stadium behind the High School to honor Doug. From the look of it, it seemed the entire town of Plymouth had come together to honor my husband.

The second memory I have is of Amanda leading the Georgia gang straight toward me. As Nathan, Rachel, Brad and Amanda moved closer, I could almost envision the armor of God gracing each frame. Nathan's sword of the Word was strapped tightly to his side, Rachel's belt of truth was donned firm and strong, Brad's breastplate of righteousness was fitted securely in place, and Amanda's feet were clad with the gospel of hope. Their helmets of salvation reminded me of Christ's gift of life, and each shield of faith was ready to encircle me (See Eph 6:10-18). They were specially fitted by God to battle any demons that dared attacked me that day.

But the demons stayed well clear of the stadium. They knew the army of God was prepared. While the Georgia gang guarded my flank, a group called the Patriot Riders surrounded the high school football field, some donning patches of American flags on their vests, other holding Old Faithful high in the air.

Each and every family of a fallen soldier not only battles grief, they also battle protesters holding banners declaring the fallen soldier deserved to die.

Erica had warned me the protesters might come and had given me the Patriot Riders website urging me to ask for their assistance. I did and they came: tough men and women motorcyclists defending freedom with American flags, black leather, chains, tattoos, and strength. If I would have met them in a dark alley I would have been terrified. That day they were the most beautiful sight I have ever seen.

Needless to say, no protesters showed up at the high school, although a few made their way into the town proper. Tony, the chief of police, quickly escorted them away.`

The Patriot Riders, the town of Plymouth, and the Georgia gang helped me stand firm while the services began. As the rain continued to fall, not heavily, but slightly, like dew from Heaven, I knew without a doubt in my soul God was crying with us.

୧୨

As soon as the services ended, Daddy started sending His answers and His warriors.

Michelle arrived first, my best friend from high school. Then came my light, Rachelle, revealing more about her dream. Each sat with me until all hours of the night, sometimes in silence, other times with tears.

Then came my rock, Tara, ready to travel across the country to discern where, if anywhere, was the right place for me to settle.

Tara was with me for five weeks, and when she left, a piece of me left with her. But on the course of our trip we hit a few places Doug and I had visited, my parents, and Columbus, Georgia. It became very clear that nothing was right, not even Columbus.

Home of the largest infantry battalion in the states, Columbus had no shortage of soldiers. Each time I saw a uniform my entire body knotted up. Every person I met in passing ultimately asked me the question I couldn't respond to without breaking down: "Is your husband in the army?"

At one point Tara looked at me and said, "What feels like home?"

I replied, "Nothing, but Plymouth feels right for now."

So I went back to Plymouth, realizing it was the one place in America I could walk down the street and have no one ask me any questions. The town had raised Doug; they already knew the answer.

Slowly, over the course of the next year, I came to know tactical unit number five. But it wasn't just Doug's family ad friends – it was an entire town.

∽

It seemed wherever I went there was someone who would offer me assistance. When tax time came around Jim stepped in to help. Although the army takes care of survivors, taxes are a monstrous tangle of uncertainties without any clear answers. But time and again Jim would look me in the eye and say, "Who is your bulldog, Nic? Me. I am your bulldog."

Then there was Cam and Dave. The first offering to mow my lawn in the summer, the latter insisting he plow my driveway in the winter. Both relieved a burden that can never be repaid.

The Biedermans, forever friends, who own a deli in Plymouth, were a constant presence in my life, bringing me smiles (and an occasional bottle of wine). They were bright lights during the long dark winters.

Support came from everywhere, and slowly, over the course of months, I knew I couldn't leave Plymouth – not yet. They were the only group of people in mass that somewhat understood.

Tactical unit number five continued to grow. Julie and Jay opened their home and became instantaneous friends. Although they left for the summer to man an ice-cream stand in New York, Julie was there when I needed her in May, the anniversary of Doug's death, when I insisted in throwing a "heavenly" birthday party.

Each year during Doug's new "birthday" bash hundreds of people from the town of Plymouth came to my house celebrating Doug's life and giving me the support I needed.

Then there was Sarah, donating part of her household goods so Dak would have a bed and toys. Within a year's time Sarah became my next-door neighbor. When I needed to cry I called Sarah and over coffee she would just be there.

Brenda came too, a faithful warrior of God, calling me when she didn't even know me. She and I had endless conversations about the coming of our Savior.

Then Roger entered my life, my forever confidant and friend, who was my sounding board for problems and a voice of resolve for my confusion. He and his daughter Cheryl welcomed me in and encouraged my faith.

In just a few short months the town of Plymouth became an army. I will be forever grateful.

∾

As time moved on, I began to feel isolated in Plymouth. Although I had made lifelong friends there visiting any of my family in the south was becoming increasingly difficult. I found myself leaving for a month here, then a month there, and I finally realized that when Dak went to school opportunities to travel would be few and far between. It was time to move.

It was a difficult decision to make but it was time. Plymouth had given me the opportunity I needed to grow strong enough to answer a stranger's question posed about Doug without collapsing in tears. It had given me the isolation I craved to sit without interruption and speak to God. The small town of three thousand had given me strength.

So with a growing four-year-old, a new cat, an old fish, and my faithful mother we closed my newly purchased house, said goodbye, and hit the road.

Destination: Columbus, Ga.

I went back to the place Doug and I felt the most at home. Now, the Battalion continues to grow.

Jessica and Monica, two wonderful friends from Germany, are now stationed in Columbus. They have continued to be a rock when I feel I am sinking.

Their husbands, Grant and Travis, stand firm when I need Dak to have a male influence. I know I can call them at a moment's notice.

Rachel and Nathan are still at the church I attended back in 2003. Their friendship has made it possible to enlist even more into the battalion. They both continue to stand as beacons of loyalty to my husband and family.

Amanda and Brad are also still in Columbus, and Amanda's smile and support continues to be a huge blessing to me. She is there for me when I need her most. As soon as I moved to Columbus, she welcomed me to her weekly Bible study group where beautiful, faithful women attend. Amanda and the women's Bible study continuously offer their prayers and support. Thank you all for putting up with my obsession about the end times.

Jake and Amanda are also a constant presence in my life. Although they are always on the move in the army, we make it a high priority to see each other as much as we can. I love you both very much.

Only through Daddy can I stand, but at times the battalion supports my weight.

I thank each and every one of you for being God's soldiers. May you shine like the stars forever and ever.

Amen and Amen! Come quickly, Lord Jesus!

Nic

Notes

All scripture quoted from the NIV Bible unless otherwise noted. In the text I have chosen to capitalize Him and He, etc, when referring to God. The NIV Bible does not do this and therefore, in the quoted scriptures, these words are not capitalized.

Chapter 1: Forsaken
1. Revelation 6:10 paraphrased
2. Psalm 8:4
3. See Matthew 25:23
4. See Revelation 22:20
5. See Revelation 6:12-13, Joel 2:30-32, and I Corinthians 15:51-53
6. See Psalm 141:2
7. Luke 18:7-8a
8. Zephaniah 3:17
9. Matthew 27:46b
10. Psalm 50:15 ESV
11. See I Thessalonians 4:16
12. See Revelation 21:14, 19-21
13. Revelation 4:8b
14. See Matthew 18:10
15. See Hebrews 12:1
16. Revelation 6:10 paraphrased

Chapter 2: Preparations
1. Check out www.grief.com/the-five-stages-of-grief
2. I Peter 5:7
3. I Kings 19:11-13a
4. Matthew 6:26
5. Psalm 139:7-10
6. Matthew 7:9-11

7. Revelation 21:23a
8. See I Kings 6:7
9. See Revelation 21:16
10. If you want to research more on Heaven, check out Randy Alcorn's *Heaven* published by Eternal Perspective Ministries in 2004. It is worth the read!
11. See Judges 13-16

Chapter 3: Questions
1. Romans 1:20
2. Revelation 22:12
3. Revelation 21:3b-4
4. Song of Songs 8:6b-7a

Chapter 4: Messages from Hell
1. Revelation 22:7a
2. Isaiah 53:6
3. Galatians 3:27
4. 2 Corinthians 5:17
5. See Psalm 139:13
6. Revelation 7:10b

Chapter 5: Messages from Heaven
1. Revelation 7:10b
2. I Corinthians 13:13
3. Check out Josh Joplin Band's Boxing Nostalgic, by Joplin Records 1998.
4. Lamentations 3:22
5. Proverbs 3:3-4
6. Psalm 34:18

Chapter 6: Our Journey
1. Check out Franklin Graham's *The Name*, published in Nashville by Thomas Nelson in 2002.
2. Isaiah 43:1b-3a
3. Isaiah 53:5-6
4. See Revelation 22:1-2
5. See Daniel 12:10

6. Check out Henry T. Blackaby and Claude V. King's *Experiencing God: Knowing and Doing the Will of God.* It is a workbook published in 1990 by Lifeway Press.
7. See Daniel 10:11
8. See Revelation 13:1-3, 17:10-11. You might also want to check out Walid Shoebat's *God's War on Terror* published in 2008 by Top Executive Media and Joel Richardson's *Antichrist: Islam's Awaited Messiah* published in 2006.
9. Revelation 13:4b
10. Ephesians 1:17 expounded

Chapter 7: Wait
1. See Daniel 12:10
2. See Matthew 24:4-14, John 16:2
3. See Revelation 4:6-8
4. Matthew 24:32-33
5. See Revelation 4:2-3
6. Revelation 4:7
7. Check out The Original TV Classic *Cricket on the Hearth* (1967 by Classic Media)
8. Proverbs 2:3-5
9. See I Thessalonians 5:17
10. Isaiah 62:11
11. Psalm 37:7
12. Luke 18:7 NCV
13. See Revelation 20
14. Revelation 21:4
15. I Peter 5:10 NCV
16. See Genesis 3:8-9
17. Genesis 1:28b
18. See Genesis 2:17
19. Isaiah 26:19
20. See Revelation 13:6
21. Revelation 21:2-3
22. Joel 2:3b NASB
23. One of my favorite Bible teachers, Beth Moore, says this all the time. This is a shout out to her. Glory!

24. See Joel 2:3b, Matthew 19:28, and Acts 3:21. If you want to see miraculous depictions of why we can believe dragons, or dinosaurs, walked with man, check out *Untold Secrets of Planet Earth* by Vance Nelson, published by Untold Secrets of Planet Earth Publishing Company, Red Deer, Alberta, Canada in 2011.
25. See Matthew 19:4-6
26. See Malachi 2:15
27. See Ephesians 5:31-32
28. Genesis 2:24
29. See Isaiah 11:6-9, 65:22-23
30. Genesis 1:28b
31. See Revelation 21:4
32. Luke 9:24
33. Matthew 22:23-28
34. Matthew 22:29-32
35. See I Corinthians 6:3
36. I Thessalonians 4:16-17a
37. John 14:2-3
38. Revelation 19:11, 14
39. See 2 Peter 3:10
40. Malachi 3:2-3a
41. See Joel 2:3b, Matthew 19:28, and Acts 3:21. Jesus and Peter actually mention the "renewal" and "restoration" of all things. Cool stuff!
42. See 2 Samuel 6:14, Psalm 139:7-10 and Song of Songs
43. See Revelation 21
44. Romans 6:23
45. See Revelation 20:8b
46. See Revelation 20:7-10
47. See Revelation 21:4
48. Genesis 1:28b

Chapter 8: The Train
1. 2 Peter 3:3-4a
2. See Ezekiel 37
3. Taken from Josh McDowell's *A Ready Defense* (San Bernardino: Here's Life Publishers, 1992).
4. See Zechariah 12:3

5. Luke 21:28b
6. Luke 21:32
7. See Matthew 16:2-3
8. Isaiah 40:3b-5
9. Robin Mark, Revival in Belfast (2003 by Sony).
10. Better Days by Bruce Springsteen is from the album Lucky Town which was released in 1992 by Sony.
11. Revelation 4:8b
12. Revelation 5:2b
13. See John 1:1 and John 14:6
14. Revelation 5:12b
15. Revelation 5:13b paraphrased

Chapter 9: Under Enemy Attack
1. I Peter 5:8-9a
2. See Hebrews 11:10
3. Psalm 91:4
4. See Isaiah 43:1-3
5. See Luke 22:31
6. James 1:6b-8
7. See Judges 15:15
8. See Joshua 1:9

A Future Chapter. . . The Opening of the Seals
1. See 2 Thessalonians 2:1-4
2. Revelation 5:12b
3. See Revelation 6:1-2, Daniel 9:27
4. See Daniel 7:8,11,25
5. Please check out Walid Shoebat's God's War on Terror published in 2008 by Top Executive Media and Joel Richardson's Antichrist: Islam's Awaited Messiah published in 2006.
6. Romans 8:38-39
7. See Revelation 6:3-4
8. See John 16:2
9. See Ephesians 6:10-18
10. Matthew 6:19-21
11. See Daniel 12:3,10

12. See Revelation 6:5-8
13. Revelation 6:6b, Daniel 9:27 – According to Daniel, most scholars believe the Jewish Temple will be rebuilt during the beginning of the final seven years on Earth. A critical component of temple worship is the oil and the wine. Both oil and wine were poured out with the daily morning and evening sacrifice. See Numbers 28:4-8
14. See John 14:6
15. See Matthew 24:1-13 and Revelation 2 and 3
16. See Revelation 6:8
17. See Revelation 12:13-17 and Revelation 13:16-17
18. See Matthew 19:5
19. John 10:27-28
20. Matthew 6:33a
21. Hebrews 13:5b Amplified Bible
22. Psalm 17:6
23. Isaiah 25:9
24. Isaiah 25:8
25. John 6:40
26. See I Corinthians 13:8, and Song of Songs 8:6
27. See Romans 8:38-39
28. Revelation 6:10b
29. See I Thessalonians 4:16-18
30. See Genesis 50:20 and Romans 8:28-29
31. See John 10:27-28
32. See Isaiah 43:1-3
33. Joshua 1:9b
34. Philippians 3:14
35. Proverbs 3:3-4
36. I Thessalonians 4:16-18

A Future Chapter. . . The Sixth Seal
1. See Revelation 13:16-17
2. See Isaiah 24:19-20
3. See Revelation 6:12, Joel 2:31
4. See Isaiah 52:12b
5. See Matthew 25:6
6. See Revelation 7:17

7. Revelation 15:3b-4a
8. See Revelation 8, 9 and 16

Then End. . . or the Beginning
1. See Revelation 19:11-13
2. See 2 Peter 3:10 and Revelation 8-9
3. See Revelation 16
4. Isaiah 60:2, See also Revelation 16:10-11
5. See Revelation 16:13-16
6. Revelation 19:6b-7

Questions

I pray you have found hope and inspiration as you have read *Revelations*. Although *Revelations* is my story, it can also be yours. Daddy can turn your tragedy into hope, your disappointments into victory, and wash your fears with His blessings. The following questions could be part of a group Bible study or a personal Bible study to help you grow closer to your Daddy and your Jesus. May His Spirit give you revelation.

Chapter I – Forsaken

1. In Chapter One, Doug's sudden death was described followed immediately with angels ushering him to Heaven. What do you think happens at the moment of death?
2. Nic tells about her thoughts and actions immediately after hearing the news of Doug's death.
   When you are faced with a tragedy or even a setback what are your first thoughts? (For some "first thoughts" in scripture read Daniel 3:8-18 and Acts 16:22-30)
3. To whom, or to where, do you turn when faced with problems that you think are beyond you? (Read Psalms 46 and 121)
4. Nic describes her concept of Heaven as she sees it, but from Doug's perspective. How do you picture Heaven? Read Revelation 21:10-27. Is this description the way you pictured it?
5. In Chapter I it seems Nic and Doug still have an awareness of each other – perhaps even a communication – an anticipation that they will be together again. Do you believe you will one day see loved ones who have passed? (Please read Hebrews 12:1 – who are the "witnesses?")

Chapter 2 - Preparations

1. "Over the prior four years my faith in God had strengthened from something I believed in to something I lived." Comment on this statement. What do think Nic means by this?
2. "I struggled with God for weeks. I yelled at Him, spewing out questions and quoting His biblical promises of love and protection. God met my questions with silence." Have you ever been angry with God or experienced God's silence? What did you then do? (read Psalms 130)
3. Samson tells Doug, "God taught Nic something, Doug. He taught her that no matter what, if you're called by God, He will use you despite your faults and your fears. He will use you even if you leave His path." Do you believe this? Have you ever experienced being used by God? Has Nic's story caused you to re-think your life experiences?
4. Doug and Samson (Judges 13-16) are talking and Samson says he always wanted to meet Doug.
   If you could meet someone from the Bible who would it be? Why? What biblical character may want to meet you?
   What biblical character do you most identify with? As in, if you were in scripture, who would you be?
5. Doug realized Nic feared disappointing God. Do you fear disappointing God? If so, how does this affect your life?

Chapter 3 – Questions

1. Before Nic arrives in Plymouth, a recent fall has placed Doug's grandmother in a nursing home. This made her house available to Nic.
   Do you think difficulties to one person can result in a blessing to another? Is this fair? How do you think God uses circumstances to weave together the tapestry of life? (read Ruth 1:1-7, 4:13-22)
2. Nic said, "I stepped on the plane with my mom, Dak, and an assisting officer, with no home and no place to call home, crawled into my seat, and cried."
   Can you imagine yourself in this position? What would you think? What would you do?
3. "Life was a choice. Choosing God was the greatest choice you could make. It was the choice everyone born should make. Yet it was a choice

many pushed aside. The Word even states that those who deny God can offer no apologies: "For since the creation of the world God's invisible qualities – his eternal power and divine nature – have been clearly seen, being understood from what has been made, so that men are without excuse" (Romans 1:20).

Have you made your choice? Have those you love? What does your/ their choice mean to you and your future? What are you going to do about it?

4. "Although Nic didn't feel like she had a home on Earth, she wasn't supposed to. There was a purpose behind his death, a purpose that in time Nic would realize. God wanted her to look up, focus her sights on His coming kingdom, and tell others. Nic would soon realize her focus was not on the life she had lost, but on the one God was saving for her when Jesus was crowned King."
   Could it be that God can turn any tragedy into a greater good? Have you experienced this? Does Nic's story help you re-think your life experiences?

5. Why was it so important to Nic for Doug's service to be in a church instead of a movie theatre?

6. Have you ever considered the rewards you would receive in Heaven? Why do you think churches don't preach about heavenly rewards? We often think of simply "Heaven" or "not Heaven" as the only possibilities. But the Bible is very clear that there are rewards for us in Heaven – it just isn't clear on exactly what those rewards will be. What will be Nic's reward? What will be Doug's reward? What do you think/hope will be your reward? Are these rewards "worth it?" (Read Revelation 22:12, Matthew 6:19-21, and Hebrews 10:35-39)

Chapter 4 – Messages from Hell

1. "A small smile crept across Doug's face as he remembered Nic sitting in their Alaskan home, reading aloud opposing views of Revelation as he made pancakes. Biblical prophecy wasn't quite what he wanted to hear on his day off, but that's when he wasn't a true believer. By the world's standards he was a good man, a model American, a loving husband, and exemplary moral leader, but that fell far short in God's eyes. He was a sinner, like everyone else. No matter how good you were by the world's

standards, it wasn't enough." Isaiah 53:6 states, "We all, like sheep, have gone astray, each of us has turned to his own way; and the Lord has laid on him the iniquity of us all."

"Are you a good person? By whose standards? How do you look to God before you come to belief? What about after?

2. "When he [Doug] delved deeper into the Word he saw the truth. Now, when God saw him, God the Father saw God the Son. 'For all of you who were baptized into Christ have clothed yourselves with Christ' (Galatians 3:27). It was a biblical promise. When you believed in the Word made flesh, you became a new creation. 'Therefore, if anyone is in Christ, he is a new creation; the old has gone, the new has come'" (2 Corinthians 5:17).

What if Doug hadn't "delved deeper into the Word" and saw the truth? Where would he then be in this story? How do we feel about "good people" in regards to salvation? Do we witness to them as forcefully as others? What changes in our attitudes? Why or why not?

3. Nic considered Doug's dog tags and wedding ring as a miracle. What miracles have happened in your life? Do you think that there may be some miracles in your life that you may have discounted as mere coincidence?

Chapter 5 – Messages from Heaven

1. Nic's friend, Rachelle, had a dream in which she saw Doug and he asked her to give a message to Nic. The Bible often tells of messages and revelation coming to a person in dreams. (read Genesis 28:10-22, Daniel 7:1-14, Matthew 1:20, 2:12-20)

Have you ever had such an experience? If so, explain. If not, do you believe this could happen? If you heard a message in a dream, would it increase your faith in God?

2. When Doug asks Jesus if he can send a message to Nic, Jesus smiled and said, "Love is stronger than death." (read Song of Songs 8:6-7) What does this mean to you?

3. "He could sense Nic's unease. She knew Heaven existed. But no one knew what eternity would bring: what would it look like, taste like, be like? Would they be together? That was her biggest fear. He had only lived thirty years on Earth, and he and Nic had only been married five of those years."

So Nic and Doug hadn't really had the opportunity to share all of life's experiences. Their life together was cut short. Does this sound like a loving God? Do you think a loving and all-powerful God has a plan for this circumstance? How do you think God could make things right in this situation? In yours? (read 2 Samuel 12:15-23)

4. "A verse in Mark 12:25 haunted her. It read, 'When the dead rise, they will neither marry nor be given in marriage; they will be like the angels in heaven.' He had been taken away too soon, Nic thought. She wanted to be with him and she didn't know if she would."

This verse haunted Nic, but after prayer and further research in God's Word, it became an inspirational revelation even though her interpretation is different from many scholars. Do you think God will give personal revelations to those who seek in order to give comfort in individual situations? Do you think perhaps God gives revelations to those who need them most?

5. "The vision of Heaven I had created wasn't the best. I think many of us are guilty of this false mentality. We think Heaven is going to be one big church service or at the very least singing praises all day long."

What is your vision of Heaven? How did you get this vision – Scripture, teachings, sermons, cartoons? What has changed?

6. "It took me months to come to the conclusion that I did, months on my knees before God with tears coursing down my cheeks. I questioned the dream and what it meant. I questioned if I understood it correctly or if I was taking something and twisting it into the response I desperately wanted to hear."

How can you know if your interpretation is correct or simply what you want to hear? (read 1 Kings 19:11-13, Acts 17:11, 22:14, John 10:3, Romans 8:14)

7. Nic tells of "accidentally" finding songs and messages from Doug.
Do you think these were coincidences? Are there things in your life that remind you of how God has spoken to you in the past?

Chapter 6 – Our Journey

1. "For God so loved the world that he gave his one and only Son, that whoever believes in him shall not perish but have eternal life." John 3:16
What does this mean to you?

2. Neither Doug nor Nic initially had positive thoughts and experiences concerning church.

   Why was this, and what changed them? Have you had a similar experience? What influences did you have in your life? How did you come to follow Christ?

3. "One day I got down on my knees after reading my Bible lesson. I remember saying through the tears, 'God, am I okay with you? I need to know if I'm okay with you.'"

   Have you ever asked this question? Did you get a response? How did that response come to you? What was the response? What did you then do?

4. Doug didn't want to take the wine of communion not because he didn't believe but because he didn't like to drink from the same cup as someone else.

   Have you ever let a "distasteful" procedure inhibit the demonstration of your faith? How about people? Did certain "Christians" turn you away or toward the Savior? How can we be a better influence to others as we walk with the Lord?

5. "In what are you investing your life, your time, and your resources? Make two lists. On the left list things that will pass away. On the right list things that have eternal value."

   Making this list helped Doug and helped Nic when she read it. Would such a list help you? Try it.

6. "I asked for wisdom as well," Daniel continued. "If you seek it, Father will never disappoint. But at times Father's revelations are isolating. When she stands for her beliefs many will question the sanity of her convictions."

   Could you stand up for your beliefs amid questions and ridicule? In the end times, scripture says many will fall away from the faith because of persecution (Matthew 24:9-10). Is your faith strong enough to survive intense persecution? The early church underwent being jailed, beaten, stoned, and tortured (see Acts 7:54-60, 12:1-4, 16:22-23, 2 Corinthians 11:23-33). Could you?

7. "God is right there, whispering to our hearts, "Believe Me; trust Me; I can do anything. One saying keeps going over and over in my mind. I believe it is from God: "Wait and see what I can do," He says. "Wait and see what I can do!""

How did this influence Nic's decisions?

When you hear from God, do you believe Him? How good are you at waiting for God? (read Isaiah 40:31, Lamentations 3:25-26, Habakkuk 2:2-3, Galations 6:9)

Chapter 7 – Wait

1. Much of Nic's concerns and decisions were based on her interpretation of "end-time" events. The Bible presents five events that are usually attributed to end time prophecy:
    *   Final seven years on Earth (some deem the "tribulation")
    *   The rapture of the church
    *   The second coming of Christ
    *   The Millennial Kingdom of Christ with believers (Satan bound)
    *   An eternal home with God

    The details, sequence and reality of these events have been debated by scholars for over 2,000 years.

    Can you believe strongly enough to make important, life changing decisions on something with conflicting opinions or no real proof?

2. "Scripture says God will make everything right. So I got to thinking; what if the millennial reign of Jesus was to right all the wrongs that had happened to God's people? Were those years a gift to us?"

    If this is true how could it affect your life and life decisions?

3. Read Genesis 1:26-2:25:

    Do you think this is representative of what God intends for us even though we have gone astray?

4. "Our life as we know it isn't over when we die. There is another phase to the believer's life. If you are crippled, you will dance. . . and live your life. If you are blind, you will see. . . and live your life. If you are insecure, you will be restored. . . and live your life. If you have miscarried a child, you will get to raise that child. . . and see that child live their life. This world cannot harm us. Why? We have the gift of the millennial reign of Christ."

    What do you think all that means for you?

5. "Then, at the end of the Millennium, Jesus will give those remaining Millennium children a final choice."

Do you think this is accurate? Why else would Satan be re-released? What about those children who have been aborted or miscarried or have died young? Do you think they are in Heaven now? (read 2 Samuel 12:22-23). Do you think they will get a choice in the Millennium, or do you believe their choice has already been made?

6. "Unfortunately, the Word says many will turn away from the absolute and total perfection of Jesus Christ on Earth. They will choose Satan." (read Revelation 20:7-10)
   Why do you think people will do that?

7. God the Father doesn't descend with the New Jerusalem until after the Millennium. Why do you think this is? (read Exodus 33:20 and Revelation 20:7-10)

8. Scripture says the "old order" will not pass away until after the Millennial Kingdom. What do you think the "old order" is? (read Revelation 21:4-5)

Chapter 8 – The Train

1. People have been predicting the end times for centuries.
   Do you see any world events that would indicate that time is really near – now? (read Daniel 12:4, 2 Tim 3:1-5, Matthew 24:4-14) Do you hope it is? Are you ready?

2. Can you imagine Heaven preparing for the return of the King? Doug seems very happy that the end is near. Do you think those who went before us are exited as well? Are you? (read Revelation 4 and 5 – this is the heavenly "before" that precedes the events of the "last days.")

3. You have just read about the worship in Heaven (Revelation 4 and 5). How and why do you worship God? What can you learn from those in Heaven?

Chapter 9 – Under Enemy Attack

1. "Submit therefore to God. Resist the devil and he will flee from you. Draw near to God and He will draw near to you." James 4:7-8a
   How do you do that – submit, resist, draw near?

2. Nic felt that Satan attacked her in the one place she thought vulnerable – her faith.

How would you describe Nic's faith in the beginning of her story? At the end of her story? If you see it changed, what caused it to change? How strong is your faith?

3. Nic said, "I have an assignment to complete."

What is her assignment? Do you have an assignment? God says you do. What is your assignment? Are you working on it? (read Ephesians 2:10)

4. What will happen when you hear the trumpet sound? Will you be taken? Or will you be left?

What can you do to prepare for the return of the King? (read I Thessalonians 5:16-24)

A Future Chapter. . . The Opening of the Seals

1. Both Nic and Doug had studied the book of Revelations and understood the sequence of events that would occur in the "end times." For some this would be frightening – for others exciting.

"Doug breathed in a special thanks to his Creator. Nic was looking up. She knew what was to come and she would tell others."

"Come," the Earth said.

"Come," the saints said.

"Come," Nic said.

"Come quickly Lord Jesus," Doug said.

He could almost feel the Earth shiver.

He wondered if Nic could feel the approaching rider.

"The train has started, Nic." Doug said. "Be strong."

Have you ever anticipated meeting a loved one that you hadn't seen in a long time – perhaps wondered if you ever would see again? And now you find you will meet. The airplane will land soon and you're at the airport waiting. Describe your emotions. Now try to speculate on your emotions if it were Jesus Christ that you were meeting. (read Revelation1:14-17)

2. "Daddy is like a parent on Christmas Eve waiting in expectation as His children wake and rush into the living room. He wants to give us that joy more than anything. He wants to surprise us with blessings and crown us with crowns. Can you imagine the day?"

Have you ever considered that God has emotions? He can be happy, sad, grieved, angry. What do you think causes those emotions in God? Do you think God is excited about the return of the King? (read Jeremiah 31:3, Luke 15:11-32)

3. "At times it seems I'm between Earth and Heaven, trying to figure out the madness of it all. Many things in this world don't make sense, but when you think about them in light of eternity, through God's eyes and not your own, peering through the Word as you study the happenings around you, in a crazy way, it slowly starts to come together."

   When you think about Doug's death "in light of eternity," do things "start to come together?" When you think of the death of your loved one "in light of eternity," do things "start to come together?" If not, what do you think would help you?

4. "The Bible is an amazing book. You can read it, know it, even memorize it, yet when certain things happen and you look at a scripture you've read a thousand times before it becomes, not something different, but something more."

   Many people start reading the Bible but quit because it is a difficult read for them. Does the statement above help you reconsider reading the Bible? (read Psalm 119:105 and John 1:14)

5. When someone asks you "How are you?" after you have experienced some difficulty, how do you respond? Nic said at times she responds by saying, "joyfully sucky." What do you think she meant by that? (read Habbakuk 3:17-19)

6. "But their Father was a romantic. He had fashioned Eve to fit Adam in the beginning and He was fashioning the bride of Christ to fit his Son in the end."

   The "bride of Christ" are those people who have chosen to follow Jesus. Why do you think the Bible uses the analogy of a bride and groom to illustrate the relationship between Christ and those that believe in Him? (read Ephesians 5:22-32 and 2 Corinthians 11:2)

7. In this chapter Nic makes statements like:

   "I can't imagine loving God any more than I do now."

   "No matter what you are going through, no matter what your mountain is, trust Daddy."

   "He [God] will take what Satan intended for harm and use it for glory."

"He has answered my prayers and has given me the strength and insight to respond to His voice."

"Thank you so much, Jesus. Thank you so much for saving my Doug." Do you wonder how she could say such things? Could you, or have you, been able to say this if you experienced a tragedy? Has Nic's story helped you understand how a person could feel this way after experiencing such a tragedy?

A Future Chapter. . . The Sixth Seal

I. "Doug wanted to say something but there were no words to describe what he was now feeling. Nic's arm encircled his neck as they soared toward the heavens, spinning in the cosmos. Then the sound of Nic's laughter, her glorious laughter, rose skyward toward the fast approaching light. As they spun and twirled, Doug saw others all around him doing the same, laughing and twirling, spinning and shouting, "Great and marvelous are your deeds, Lord God Almighty. Just and true are your ways, King of the ages. Who will not fear you, O Lord, and bring glory to your name?""
Close your eyes. Try to picture this scene in your mind. How does it make you feel? Is there anything new you are now looking forward to?

2. "The stars began to fall around them, like a glorious display of fireworks, but Doug instinctively knew the universe was now in chaos. The wrath of God had begun. It was necessary. Jesus was about to return to judge the world. Those left behind needed to repent – and quickly. God was urging them to believe and have life in the Lamb."
Again, close your eyes. Picture this scene. How does it make you feel? Which one is most appealing? How can you be certain you'll be in the first scene and not the second? (Read Revelation 8:6-13 for an image of the beginning of God's wrath.)

The End. . .Or the Beginning

I. "The horseman of the apocalypse had tread across the land, causing chaos and unrest. The trumpets had laid the Earth's surface waste and uprooted those disloyal to the kingdom of the Lamb."
Why would a loving and merciful God do this? (read Isaiah 48:9)

2. "He [Doug] could also feel Jesus' hand on his shoulder and his Savior's breath against his forehead. "You were worth it."

   How does this make you feel? Jesus would say this to each and every one of us. If this is what He would say to us, how should we live our lives?

3. "Doug's mouth lifted in a smile as he watched the Lamb move forward. Doug placed his hand over Nic's. It was time to reclaim the Earth. Then life could truly begin.

   Does this concluding statement help you understand a previous statement: "Jesus had smiled and said, 'Love is stronger than death.'" And the assurance from the Bible — "And now these three remain: faith, hope and love. But the greatest of these is love" (I Corinthians 13:13)

4. After reading *Revelations*, has your view of Heaven or the Millennium changed? How?

Made in the USA
Charleston, SC
21 August 2012